Stories in the Sky

Thomas Paul Thigpen

Stories in the Sky

Discovering
Bible pictures in the
constellations of the sky

Illustrated by Dennis Jones

Chariot Books
DAVID C. COOK PUBLISHING CO.

Chariot Books is an imprint of David C. Cook Publishing Co.

David C. Cook Publishing Co., Elgin, Illinois 60120
David C. Cook Publishing Co., Weston, Ontario

STORIES IN THE SKY
© 1986 Thomas Paul Thigpen

Illustrated by Dennis Jones
Star charts drawn by Cindy Markow
Design by Barbara Sheperd Tillman

First printing, 1986
Printed in the United States of America
90 89 88 87 86 1 2 3 4 5

Library of Congress Cataloging in Publication Data
Thigpen, Thomas Paul, 1954
    Stories in the sky.
    Bibliography: p. 155
    Includes index.
    Summary: Presents diagrams and descriptions of all the major constellations showing Biblical characters and objects rather than the classical ones. Also includes instructions for stargazing, charts showing when the constellations appear, and a variety of historical, biblical, and scientific facts.
    1. Stars—Observers' manuals—Juvenile literature. 2. Constellations—Observers' manuals—Juvenile literature. 3. Bible—Astronomy—Juvenile literature. [1. Stars—Observers' manuals. 2. Constellations—Observers' manuals. 3. Bible—Astronomy] I. Jones, Dennis, ill.   II. Title.
QB801.7.T48   1986   523.8'9   85-29109
ISBN 0-89191-361-0

To my wife, Leisa—
she put the stars in my eyes.

ACKNOWLEDGMENTS

Of all the folks who contributed somehow to the creation of this book, at least a few deserve special mention.

The great clarity, wit, and enthusiasm of H. A. Rey, which have made his books on the stars so popular, have been a great inspiration to me. As a child I loved his writings, and they've continued to be a joy over the years. I'm deeply grateful to him, and heartily recommend his work to all star watchers.

I feel a special kinship with Richard Hinckley Allen, a nineteenth-century scholar of the heavens. We share an alma mater (Yale) and a fascination with historical details which many others would find merely trivial. I wholeheartedly identify with his special interests, though I could never hope to match the quality of his research. Mr. Hinckley's comprehensive book *Star Names: Their Lore and Meaning* was a priceless resource of information and personal delight. Anyone who wants to pursue further the history of astronomy couldn't find a better place to start than with his book.

Catherine Davis and LoraBeth Norton, my editors at David C. Cook, have been a continual encouragement. I thank them for their sensitive and supportive work; this book is much richer for their contributions.

I thank Donald Tuttle, astronomer, educator, and former director of the School District U-46 Observatory and Planetarium of Elgin, Illinois, for his helpful evaluation and suggestions.

My thanks as well to Reverend Sanford V. Brown and his parish, Trinity United Methodist Church, of Savannah, Georgia. Their gracious gift of office space provided a "birthing room" for this book, and their joyful spiritual support has made me feel as if it's their "baby" as well.

A special word of gratitude to my treasured friend Carl Rowe, whose initial enthusiasm about the idea convinced me that others could be as excited as I was about the subject.

Also thanks to the young patrons of the CEL Regional Library in Savannah, Georgia, whose love for reading reminded me again and again just how much a good book can mean to a young mind.

Last and best: My love and thanks to my wife and daughter, who patiently endured both my long days at the office and my restless nights, when I couldn't sleep because I had constellations on my mind. These two ladies are the real stars of this book.

—T. P. T.

A NOTE TO PARENTS AND TEACHERS

My grandparents lived on a farm in rural Georgia, where the stars had no jealous competition from streetlights. Each summer my brothers and I took turns visiting for a week, and one of my habits on that vacation was to lie on my back each night in the yard, gazing up at the heavens.

As a city boy, I was amazed to find the country sky so much more crowded than the one I knew. Yet somehow it was lonelier as well. The comfortable patch of sky I saw from a window at home seemed hardly more than an extension of the roof. But here, the overarching firmament seemed so vast and wild, so much deeper and darker and more distant. It was terrifyingly alien. I felt like a grain of sand on the edge of a cosmic ocean, and I wondered when some stray wave of that boundless blackness might wash me away.

The only star pattern I knew then was the Big Dipper. Somehow it comforted me a little to be able to locate it there, like a familiar face in a crowd of cold and strange eyes. It was the first thing I looked for each night, and my gaze would return to it again and again, as if to make sure that my one tame outpost in that immense wilderness had not been overrun.

But then one night, I saw something else. High above the horizon, near the crown of the sky, was a brilliant star; it had always been there, but for the first time I noticed that it was not alone. Somehow my vision had at last grouped it with six others to form a shining, silver cross emblazoned on the night. I had discovered the Northern Cross.

That night my feeling about the heavens, and about the earth as well, was changed. I had been in Sunday school long enough to know the meaning of a cross, and whose unmistakable token it was. So it seemed to me in that moment as if God had branded the sky with seven white-hot irons to tell me clearly, "This, too, is mine."

The darkness was still vast and limitless, the stars too many to number. But now I knew in my imagination as well as my mind that God held it all in the palm of his hand. And if he held the heavens, he surely held the earth as well.

In years to come, I would struggle with questions of faith and knowledge; I would doubt and wonder and rebel. But even during the times when I claimed to disbelieve, I would look up at the sky some evenings, and see the Cross. It haunted me and challenged me. The heavens were telling the glory of God, and I could never quite shut out the music of their cosmic chorus.

Today I walk in faith again, and the whole sky has become a treasury of reminders about my Creator. I've learned to recognize most of the classical constellations, and I take great pleasure in tracing the patterns. But my imagination has never been content to stop at that. Just as I discovered the Northern Cross on my own, so I've discovered many other figures—some that people for thousands of years in many cultures have agreed were there, others that reflect my own pet fancies.

At the same time, I've found that a number of natural phenomena can teach us supernatural truth. The objects of nature around us are useful visual aids for lessons in faith, as Jesus himself demonstrated: "Look at the birds of the air. . . . Consider the lilies of the field. . . . Learn a lesson from the fig tree. . . ." The great canvas of creation has much to say about the wisdom and majesty and power of the Artist who has taken such delight in his work.

Thus I offer this book on how to discover Bible stories in the stars. As a Christian parent and the associate editor of a newsletter for parents, I'm anxious to find every possible avenue for teaching children about the ways of God. The "teachable moment" is often focused on some natural phenomenon that stirs a child's interest, and so I hope to help parents and teachers make the most of that fascinating cosmic text we call the night sky.

The book is designed so that older children can read and use it on their own, or younger children can have it read to them. The information is nontechnical and just sufficient to help children find their way around the sky for the pleasure of it. The emphasis is not on astronomy, but on star watching. For that reason, the great fun of this project will be to match the charts and stories with the real thing outdoors at night. And that may require your involvement. Every hour spent with your kids looking at the constellations and telling Bible stories about them will be a priceless investment for years to come.

You should know from the start that this book sits squarely in the realm of *astronomy*, not *astrology*. Christians who are rightly concerned that their children avoid tampering with horoscopes can rest assured that I have no association with any such occult practices, and have made a special effort to explain to the reader the difference between star *watching* and star *reading*. I'm saddened to realize that even the names of the twelve constellations in the zodiac have been tainted in the popular mind by occultic association. (What comes to mind, for example, when you hear the name "Aquarius"?) My growing conviction is that our imaginations need to recapture these good gifts of God for his glory.

At the same time, I have no intention of trying to "replace" the Greek mythological figures that have come down to us as the traditional constellations. That was tried on several occasions by Christian astronomers hundreds of years ago, but the popular pictures were simply too deeply ingrained to be given up so easily.

My goal is much more modest. I want to help children realize that these star patterns have been recognized and named by many different cultures in many different ways. No one has a monopoly on them. Though they'll probably want to learn the classical constellations some time as well, I want them to know they are free to find many other exciting pictures in the heavens. If they start with this book, they'll have the pleasure of finding some familiar Bible stories in the sky.

Meanwhile, the value of the resulting fun, the gain in scriptural knowledge, and the enrichment of imagination will be hard to calculate. In this particular activity, the sky is quite literally the limit!

Thomas Paul Thigpen

CONTENTS

I
WHY WATCH THE STARS?

A GIANT PICTURE BOOK

Suppose that the sky were totally dark for most of our lives. One night every hundred years, the stars appeared. Would you and your family stay up that night to see them?

Of course! And so would most of the world. In fact, you would probably take pictures and make careful notes of what you saw, so you could tell your children and grandchildren about it someday. Enjoying such a beautiful sight would be a special privilege you would always treasure.

Now think about the world as it really is. That glorious sight you would stay up all night to enjoy once in a lifetime is available to you *every* night the sky is clear. But we've grown so familiar with the great beauty of the stars that most of us rarely even bother to look up. We forget to be excited as King David was, who as a shepherd boy knew what it was like to camp out under a breathtaking sky: "The heavens declare the glory of God," he sang. "The skies proclaim the work of his hands" (Psalm 19:1).

How Many Do *You* Know?

Though we may tend to take the stars for granted this way, we're still not as familiar with them as we may think. You can look at a map of America and locate a number of states just by their shape, but how many stars can you name and locate on a map of the night sky? How many of the groups of stars called *constellations* (those that form imaginary pictures in the sky) can you name and locate? Could you find any of those constellations just by going out and looking for them at night?

If not, you're missing a great treat. The night sky is like a giant picture book, with shining outlines of heroes and rascals, animals and objects, all fitting together in fascinating patterns that will tell a story, if you let them. The purpose of this book is to help you learn to recognize those characters and remember their stories. All you need to enjoy the sky in this way are the book in your hands, a flashlight to read by, and a place for viewing the sky without trees or buildings in the way.

17

A New Set of Constellations

Even if you are familiar with the night sky, you've probably never thought of looking for the constellations pictured in this book. They're not the ones you'll find in other books about the stars. Most of the star pictures that books show today have come down to us from the ancient Greeks, who lived many hundreds of years ago. These and some others are considered the "official" constellations, and you may know some of their names: Pisces the Fish, for example, or Leo the Lion, or Taurus the Bull.

You may be surprised, however, to find that these Greek constellations are not the only ones, nor are they even the oldest. Two hundred years before Christ, the Greek star watcher Hipparchus wrote that the constellations he used weren't the same ones passed down to him from the generation before. And he questioned whether the generation before had used the ancient pictures without making their own changes. So Hipparchus's rule was to use the figures that most closely looked like the star groups as they appeared.

Other cultures had their own schemes. We have discovered through historical records from around the world that many other ancient peoples looked up at the sky and made their own pictures, including the Hebrew people of the Old Testament.

The point, then, is this: Though it's useful to learn the Greek constellations as we study the sky, we're free to discover as well whatever patterns we can. We may use our own imaginations. In this book, you'll find a collection of constellations that represent characters and objects from the Bible. God wants us to enjoy the beauty he made in the night sky. As we look at the immense, distant objects of light we call stars, it's easy to be reminded of God's power and greatness. So why not connect our star pictures with stories about God and his people, to help us remember the wonderful things he has done?

With that in mind, let's take a closer look at how stars and constellations came to be named, and see what the Bible has to say about the stars. Then we'll go over some tips for star watching, get acquainted with the night sky, and jump right in. The charts and descriptions you find here will introduce you to the sky's cast of fascinating characters one at a time. Soon you'll be reading the Bible stories written across the sky, made by God for us to enjoy.

HOW THE STARS GOT THEIR NAMES

Before the invention of electric lights, the nights were darker and more mysterious. There were no streetlamps to blot out the stars, so the sky looked like diamonds scattered through a bed of coal.

The stars were familiar sights to everyone then, but most especially to travelers, who used them as signposts in the sky. The stars helped people find their way across unknown seas and deserts, where everything else was unfamiliar.

Ancient peoples also told time by the sky. The sun and certain stars showed them the correct time of the day or month. The moon told the time of month. And the stars measured out the seasons and years.

In many places, planting and harvesting were planned around the movements of the moon, stars, and planets. The Hebrew people had a calendar based on the moon and the sun, and it was used to schedule many agricultural, social, and religious events in their society.

According to the Bible, God had some of these uses in mind when he made the stars. Although these great, glowing balls of gas are billions of miles away from us, making us feel tiny and unimportant by comparison, yet the Lord chose to arrange them in a way that would serve "for signs, and for seasons" (Genesis 1:14, KJV). It should humble us to know that God has harnessed even the most majestic of his creations for our help and pleasure.

19

That Reminds Me of Something. . . .

In all these ways, then, stars have been important to people from the very beginning. But no one knows who first looked up at the night sky and said, "That group of stars *reminds* me of something. . . ." We do know, however, that in some of our oldest historical records—clay tablets from Mesopotamia, the pyramids in Egypt, and statues from Greece—people were already calling groups of stars by special names.

We also know that the ancient Hebrews had such constellations, though we're not sure what many of them were like. Several writers of long ago claimed that Noah, Enoch, Seth, and Adam himself knew about constellations. They believed that God allowed men like Methusaleh to live so long (Genesis 5:27 says he died at the age of 969) because he wanted them to have lots of time to study the stars! We don't know whether or not that's true. But we can be certain that constellations have been around for centuries.

Some of the star patterns in the sky look so much like a familiar object that they were given the same names by different peoples who knew nothing of one another's cultures. One constellation, for example, is a long, winding ribbon of stars. Almost everyone around the world has agreed that this group looks like a river—

though in Egypt it was called the Nile; in Mesopotamia, the Euphrates; and in Italy, the Po (after real rivers in each of these lands).

The constellation known as Virgo is another good example. It was said to look like a woman in such widely distant places as ancient China, India, Assyria, Egypt, Greece, and Scandinavia. That's a convincing list of agreeing experts!

But it's hard to see how some of the other constellations got their popular names. *Canis Minor,* for instance, means Little Dog, but its two lonely stars look like only the shining eyes of a puppy. *Ursa Major,* the Great Bear, was given that name in many cultures. But it has a long tail, and doesn't really look much like a bear. Some ancient tribes said it was a wagon instead.

In any case, a number of constellation names eventually became popular among the ancient Greeks, and then the Romans after them, who spread their culture all around the Western part of the world. Many of these names have been handed down to us today. Others were added by modern astronomers. In 1930 the International Astronomical Union set up an official scheme that would be used around the world. In this scheme, eighty-eight constellations cover the sky, though we can't see all of them at once. Some of them can never be seen from our latitude in the northern hemisphere.

Individual Star Names

Most individual stars have Arabic rather than Greek names. The Arabs have been great admirers of the night sky for many centuries, partly because in times past they depended so much on the stars to guide them in the desert. When much of the ancient Greek and Roman learning was lost in Europe during the so-called Dark Ages, Arab scholars were careful to preserve what they had learned, and added much more as well to the science of *astronomy* (the study of the heavenly bodies). So we still use many of the names they gave to individual stars.

If you don't already know the official names of the more common constellations, you'll find that information useful when you're talking with others about the stars. So in each constellation description we give in this book, you'll find the official name given at the end.

You'll also find two useful lists at the end of the book. One gives the official Latin names of all the constellations in alphabetical order, along with the biblical names we've given them. The other gives the biblical names in alphabetical order, with their Latin names beside. That way, whichever name you have in mind for a star group—the official or the biblical name—you can find the other name quickly.

For now, though, you can concentrate on the fun of learning about several dozen Bible characters that fit the patterns quite well. Then you can go on, if you like, to make up your own as well. But don't be surprised if an idea you thought *you* were the first to have was already on the books in China three thousand years go!

STARS IN THE BIBLE

The Bible is as full of stars as a clear summer night. In its very first chapter, Genesis 1, we read that God made the stars and called them "good." In its very last chapter, Revelation 22, we hear Jesus saying, "I am the bright Morning Star." Between these two verses, we can find a number of passages that suggest how important stars were to the people of the Bible.

The Stars, God's Creation

Most verses that mention the stars talk about them as a whole. They remind us that God created them, has counted them, and even has a name for each of them (see Psalm 147:4). The Bible also tells us that just as the Lord scattered the stars across the sky in creation, he will gather them back together again on judgment day, when they will turn dark and fall (Matthew 24:29).

The Scripture says as well that the stars speak of God's glory (Psalm 19:1-4). Just by looking at them, people are moved to wonder at his creative power. The psalmist encourages the stars to praise God in their own special way—to tell how great he is by the very fact of their beauty, in the same way a beautiful picture brings praise to the artist who painted it (Psalm 148:3).

The Stars in God's Promises

Stars are important in several promises from God. When the Lord told Abraham that he would give him many descendants, he told him to count the stars—because Abraham's children would be just as numerous (Genesis 15:5). That may be the reason ancient Jewish legend claims Abraham was famous for his observations of the sky—he would have had to examine it carefully to make that kind of a count!

In Daniel, God promises that "those who lead many to righteousness [will shine] like the stars for ever and ever" (Daniel 12:3, NIV). In Peter's second letter, he says that if you pay attention to the Bible, the "morning star" will rise in your heart (II Peter 1:19) and cause you to understand God's Word. Finally, as we mentioned before, Jesus calls himself the Morning Star, who announces that the dawn of God's promised salvation has come to the world (Revelation 22:16).

The Stars As Poetry

Stars are often used as poetic symbols in Scripture because they are a familiar image to people everywhere. When the apostle Paul tells Christians that they live in a spiritually dark generation, he reminds them that the light of Christ's life in them makes them shine out against the blackness like stars (Philippians 2:15, 16). This is a beautiful picture that people of every culture can appreciate.

At the same time, the Devil is described poetically by Isaiah as a once-beautiful star who tried to raise himself up in pride above God's throne, but was cast down instead like a meteor (Isaiah 14:12-15). This powerful image of a "falling star" is a frightening reminder that even a beautiful creation of God can turn away from him and lose its proper place in his order.

Star Groups in the Bible

Only a few specific groups of stars are mentioned in Scripture by name, all in the Old Testament. We're not exactly sure, however, which constellations these Hebrew words are talking about.

As far as Bible scholars can tell, the three groups that appear in Job 38:31, 32 (and are mentioned in a few other places) are these: the *Pleiades*, a beautiful cluster of faint stars that looks like a silver cloud in the middle of the constellation called the Bull; a constellation called the Giant in many ancient cultures, whose official name now is *Orion*; and the *Bear*, the constellation which surrounds the Big Dipper.

The Stars As Signs

The Bible tells us that the heavenly bodies are to serve as signs, and so they have for thousands of years. Mankind has made use of their regular movements and positions to determine the weather, mark the calendar, and find directions.

But the stars can be signs in another way as well. God sometimes uses unusual events in the sky to make an announcement, such as when the star appeared over Bethlehem to proclaim the birth of his Son. Jesus talks about this kind of special announcement when he predicts that in the last days before he returns, there will be "signs in the sun, moon, and stars" (Luke 21:25).

In light of Jesus' words, it's understandable that down through the ages, many Christians have tended to look at every unusual event in the sky as a sign of the end of the world. Halley's comet is a good example of such an unusual sky event—though of course we know now that it's a regular visitor. This comet has frequently spurred people into strange behavior, because they were convinced when it appeared that the judgment day was near.

Needless to say, people who thought the end of the world was predicted in the sky at one time or another have always been mistaken . . . so far. For that reason, we must be careful not to read messages in the sky that aren't there. This is particularly important when we see what the Bible says about *astrology*, the attempt to foretell the future by studying the regular movements of the planets and stars. (This ancient craft is not to be confused with *astronomy*, which is simply the scientific study of heavenly bodies.)

Thousands of years ago, astrology was practiced by pagan peoples who came into contact with Israel. Sadly enough, some Israelites, too, began to put their hope for a happy future in the stars, instead of trusting in the God who made the stars. Some even worshiped the stars, as if they had some power to help people or to change the course of history (II Kings 17:16).

This grieved and angered God deeply, for his people should have known better. He had even warned them, when he gave Moses the Law, that they

That should be warning enough for us as well. Astrology in any form is really just an attempt to take care of our own future instead of going to God as our only hope. The stars have no power to determine history; that power belongs to the Lord alone. So remember as you use this book that our desire will always be simply to *watch* the stars and enjoy them—never to *read* their movements as keys to our future.

Knowledge in the Skies

To sum up, then, the Bible shows us that stars are an important part of creation, though we must never worship them or trust them to direct our actions. God himself has called them good, and has thought enough of them to give each one its own name. He arranged them in a way that their positions and movements would help people in measuring time and distance. His Word has also made use of their majestic beauty to talk about spiritual truths.

Finally, God speaks to us through the stars themselves. Occasionally he has spoken through special signs in the sky, but more often through the simple fact that they are there. Their awesome size and loveliness reflect his power and creativity.

must not bow down to the stars (Deuteronomy 4:19). Through the prophet Isaiah, God told the people once more that if they trusted in the predictions of astrologers, they would be ruined (Isaiah 47:13). He warned them through Jeremiah that they shouldn't learn this worthless and misleading pagan art, or be terrified by the so-called signs that the astrologers saw in the sky (Jeremiah 10:2, 3).

This last truth about the stars is the one that should mean the most to us as we begin to look at the sky. Each time we find a Bible story in the constellations, and think about the glorious lights God has placed there, we can agree gratefully with David that "night after night [the heavens] display knowledge" of the Lord (Psalm 19:2). That's the kind of knowledge we all need—so let's go on now to consider some practical tips for star watching.

TIPS FOR STAR WATCHING

If you had lived in Jesus' time, you probably wouldn't have needed any tips for sky watching. Most parents then taught their children about the stars just as parents today teach them about street signs, because the information could be necessary for survival. If you were lost at night, the stars might be your only method of finding your way.

Because there were few cities then—and no electric lights or thick smog—you would not have had to worry much about finding the right place to sky watch. Unless you lived in a dense forest, the heavens over your home were broad and clear (except, of course, for clouds).

Today, however, we depend on maps, highway signs, and information desks to find our way. Our upward view is usually crowded with buildings and hazy with pollution, and electric light gives us a kind of man-made daytime even at midnight. Though it's true you can look up anywhere outdoors and see *some* stars, anyone who wants to make a hobby of it can use a few pointers on getting the best view. Here are some guidelines to keep in mind.

The Best Places to Watch

No matter where you live—city, suburb, or country—you can see at least some stars at night if the sky isn't cloudy. But you'll see fewer stars when you observe near bright lights or in a haze or smog. The reason for this is that you're viewing the stars through miles and miles of air containing water droplets, dust and smoke particles, and other substances. The more particles there are, the more light from other sources will be reflected back to blot out the fainter stars.

If you live in the city, you need to take special precautions to make sure you have the best possible view. First of all, try to choose a place where streetlights, buildings, or trees don't get in the way of too much sky. In general, the higher the better; so if you can, go out on the roof of an apartment or office building. If you can't avoid bright lights altogether, try to position yourself so that buildings screen them out some. You may see less of the sky, but the part you do see will show more stars.

If you live in the suburbs or country, your problems will be simpler. You can probably just go out in your backyard, or better yet to a pasture or school playground. Once again, if a streetlight is a problem, try to stand where a tree or house blocks it.

Wherever you observe, don't strain too hard to see constellations when they're very low on the horizon. The atmosphere near the ground is more dense than it is higher up. A ground haze often blots out fainter stars and makes bright ones look dimmer. If possible, wait till the constellation is higher in the sky (some of the charts in this book will tell you when).

The Best Times to Watch

Wherever you live, nights with clear skies are, of course, best for observing. Remember, too, that while the full moon is beautiful, it steals the show. Unless you want to watch the moon itself (certainly a worthwhile activity), try to choose a moonless or near-moonless night. In the city, air pollution levels are lowest after a good stiff wind or heavy rain has cleansed the air.

But even if there are a few clouds or a little moonlight, you can still see a good number of stars. In fact, trying to make out constellations when parts of them are hidden makes the challenge more entertaining.

Different times of the year have their advantages and disadvantages for sky watching. Winter nights are often dry and clear, and therefore excellent for observing. Air pollution is usually less in the winter than in the summer. In addition, darkness comes earlier in the winter, so you can see the stars right after supper, and stay out longer.

The obvious disadvantage of the winter is the cold! If you bundle up well, though, and bring some extra blankets, winter star watching is well worth the price of numb fingers and toes.

Summer nights are much more comfortable, and when the air is dry, the stars may be quite brilliant. But darkness comes much later—as late as nine or ten o'clock in some places.

To see the most stars on any night, it's best to wait until at least an hour after sunset, when the sky has completely darkened. But when you're first starting out to learn the constellations, you may want to come out earlier, because only the planets and brighter stars will be showing. That way you won't be confused by many fainter stars. Later in the evening, when you're better acquainted with the sky, the dimmer stars will appear.

Keep in mind that the constellations you'll be able to see depend on the season of the year and the time of the evening. To see a particular star group, you may have to wait until a later hour or even a later month. So if you want to get acquainted with them all, you should go out as often as you can in all the seasons.

What to Take with You

The stars of the constellations in this book can all be seen with the naked eye if the night is dark and clear, so you won't need any fancy equipment.

In fact, field glasses and telescopes are better left inside when you're looking at constellations, because they narrow your field of vision too much. They're better used when looking closely at the moon, a planet, or a star cluster.

You'll need a flashlight so you can read the charts, but if you don't dim it in some way, it will keep your eyes from adjusting to the dark. Red light is best, so try covering the end of the flashlight with red tissue paper or cellophane. You could even paint it with red fingernail polish. If you can't make it red, at least dim it by covering the end with a handkerchief.

Bring a blanket, or perhaps a lounge chair so you can lie back on the ground. This is important: If you try to star watch with your head bent upward, your vision will not be as accurate and your neck will get stiff!

Now that you have your props, there's only one thing left to do. Wait until dark! Then you'll be ready to get acquainted with the night sky.

GETTING ACQUAINTED WITH
THE NIGHT SKY

At last the sun has set, and you've found just the right place to watch the sky. About two thousand visible stars are waiting for you. What's the first thing you do? Close your eyes!

That may sound odd, but it's true. The reason is that your eyes need to adjust themselves to the darkness in order to see the fainter stars. So lie down and close your eyes. Then count slowly to one hundred and ninety-nine, keeping your eyes shut. Now open them and look up. The bright stars will look brighter, and many more dim stars will now be visible.

Once your eyes are adapted this way, don't look directly at the flashlight, a streetlamp, or any other bright light. If you do, you'll lose your dark adaptation quickly.

Star Movements

If you watch long enough, you may notice that the stars seem to move very gradually across the sky. Some appear to circle counterclockwise around a star in the northern sky, called Polaris or the Polestar or the North Star. Others seem to rise in the east and set in the west. Later in the night, in fact, some of the stars that were above the horizon before will be hidden below it, while others will appear that were hidden before. They make one complete trip every twenty-four hours (minus four minutes).

Actually, it's not the stars that are moving, but the earth. Our planet, of course, spins around on its *axis*—an imaginary line through its center, from North Pole to South Pole. The spinning

29

turns us away from some stars and toward others. The result is that they seem to move, just as the sun seems to move during the day. The Polestar appears not to move, however, because it is almost directly above the earth's north axis of rotation, which is called the pole of the sky.

To get a picture of this movement, imagine a giant umbrella. The Polestar is at its center, other stars are scattered out around the spokes, and you are lying at the end of the handle. As the umbrella slowly turns, you see the other stars going around the Polestar at the center. Again, it's not really the stars that are turning; we are. So if you want to, you can imagine that the umbrella is lying still and you're turning around.

In addition to spinning on its axis, of course, the earth also moves around the sun, making one complete trip each year. This changes the look of the skies as well, hiding different constellations below the horizon every month. That's why some of them are visible only at certain times of the year.

The six constellations near the Polestar are called *circumpolar constellations.* They may be high or low in the sky as they travel around the Polestar, but in most parts of the United States (except in Florida and Hawaii) they are always above the horizon. They never rise or set, and can be seen at any time of the year.

The constellations farther from the pole—which is the great majority of them—go below the horizon as they travel around the pole. A great number of them can only be seen for part of

the night, and in any particular month some of them cannot be seen at all. In fact, some of the constellations can *never* be seen from our part of the world, because they make their whole turn below the horizon. To see them, you have to travel far south to some place like Australia or Argentina.

If all these nightly and monthly movements of the stars sound confusing, don't worry. The charts in this book will tell you when and where certain ones can be seen best. No

On the other hand, the planets of our solar system (like Venus, Mars, and Jupiter) are *not* fixed in their relation to the rest of the heavenly bodies. Their orbit around the sun takes them in a different direction. In fact, the name planet comes from a Greek word that means wanderer. The planets appear to roam around the sky, from constellation to constellation. So they were once called wandering stars.

That means that planets can't be depended on to find any particular star group. Instead, they actually get in the way of beginning star watchers because they can be mistaken for stars and make a constellation look as if it has an extra member. So if you come across a brilliant star in a constellation that doesn't appear in the chart, it's probably a planet.

The way to tell planets from stars is to remember that real stars twinkle unless they're directly overhead. Planets shine with a steadier light and are much brighter than most of the stars. Anywhere from one to four of them may be in the sky throughout the night.

matter which constellations may be hidden on a particular night, you can be sure that there will be others visible for you to enjoy.

Watch Out for Planets!

Though the stars as a whole move across the sky together, they don't change their position in relation to each other. For this reason, we call the stars fixed stars—they are fixed in place beside one another.

In the Bible, the letter of Jude warned Christians of long ago that people would come into the church who didn't really know God. They would teach things that weren't true, and mislead the sincere Christians in the church. To paint a picture of this situation, Jude called these people wandering stars (Jude 13). By this he meant that, like the planets, they wandered around in errors instead of holding fast to the truth, often causing people to lose their way.

If you come across a planet, you can recognize it for what it is and enjoy its beauty. But at the same time, let it remind you to beware of spiritual "wandering stars" who might lead you away from God. Always let the great shining truth of God's Word be a fixed "Polestar" to show you the way.

Finding the Polestar

Because the Polestar doesn't move, it has special importance. It's the star sailors have always used to find their way; no matter where they were, it told them which way was north. For the same reason, the Polestar is useful in helping you locate constellations. Each time you set out to find a particular star group, you can begin by looking for the Polestar.

How do you find the Polestar? It's easy. Do you know where the Big Dipper is? Most people have learned to recognize this group of seven stars shaped like a cup with a ladle. If you can't find it, ask almost anyone to show it to you. Or find out which direction is north, and look in that general area for seven stars that look like the illustration on this page.

Once you spot the Big Dipper, focus on the two stars that form the end of the bowl farthest from the handle. Now, in your imagination, draw a line between these two stars, and extend it about five times as long beyond the mouth of the bowl. This imaginary line will run into the Polestar. You can't miss it; there are no bright stars near it. (The two stars in the Big Dipper that you

used are called the *Pointers*, because they always point to the Polestar.)

If you face the Polestar, you are facing north. To your right is east, to your left is west, and behind you is south. If you ever lose your way at night, you can find the directions without the help of a compass!

Take Your Time

Now that you know how to find the Polestar, you're ready to learn about the rest of the sky. As you look, remember that the patterns in the sky will be much bigger than the pictures in this book. Take your time. If you can't find the constellation you want, try looking without turning your head; just shift your eyes. Stick to the small part of the sky where you're searching until you find the group.

If you become discouraged, just stop looking and enjoy the sky as a whole, or make up some constellations of your own. Spend a few minutes thanking God for the stars and praising him for their beauty. You can look again tomorrow night, or perhaps a family member or friend can help you look.

Be patient. If you locate just one or two constellations each evening, you're doing fine. It will take a whole year to see all the constellations that will pass overhead . . . so relax and enjoy them!

II
LEARNING THE CONSTELLATIONS

HOW TO USE THE BIBLICAL CONSTELLATION CHARTS

In the official set of constellations, there are eighty-eight groups. About sixty of these can be seen from our half of the world (the northern hemisphere), but we never see them all at once. Only about two dozen are visible at any given moment.

A few constellations that are very faint and uninteresting have not been included in this collection. Others have been combined to form a single figure. So on the following seventeen charts you'll find sixty-four biblical constellations. If you learn even thirty of the important ones, you'll have a good working knowledge of the sky.

The constellations are presented in charts, a few at a time. You can read some notes of interest about their connection to Scripture, other names they've had in history, and a few facts about their most important stars. Study the pictures until you're familiar with them. Once you know their shapes, it's much easier to find them in the sky when night comes.

It's important to remember that only the stars themselves, and not the lines drawn between them, will be visible in the sky! Many books on constellations show elaborate figures drawn around the stars. They are attractive, but they don't look anything like what you actually see when you look up. For that reason, we've kept our pictures very basic, with only simple lines,

curves, and circles. The resulting figures may look a little like dot-to-dot drawings, but that's the idea!

The particular constellations we're talking about on each page will be surrounded by white. This is to set them apart from the others that are shown nearby to let you know who are "neighbors." The numbers next to each neighboring constellation tell you in which charts they can be found.

The charts have an indicator of compass directions: north, south, east, and west. On maps of the earth's surface, when north is up, east is to the right and west is to the left. On sky maps, however, when north is up, east is to the *left* and west is to the *right*. That's because earth maps show the ground you're standing on, while sky maps show what's overhead. If you lie down and hold a chart over your head, with north pointing the right way, the other directions will fall into place.

One final note about directions. In our descriptions of the constellations, keep in mind this simple rule. When we're looking at a human figure, the terms "right" and "left" will mean the figure's *own* right and left, not ours. This is important, because some characters are turned upside down in the sky from our viewpoint, and right and left could be confused. But if Goliath, for example, is right side up to us, his right leg will be on the *left* side of the drawing in the chart, if he's facing us. This may all be confusing now, but it should be more clear when you begin using the charts.

From time to time, as we talk about the brightest stars in the sky, we'll compare their size and their *luminosity* to our own sun. The size we talk about will always be *diameter*, or the distance across. Luminosity means the amount of light the star gives off, not how bright it appears to us on earth. For example, when we say the star *Spica* is five times the size of the sun, we mean it's five times as large *across*. When we say it's 1,000 times as luminous, we mean that the amount of light it gives off is 1,000 times as much as that from the sun. (If it were 1,000 times as bright in the sky, we'd all be blinded by it.)

Distances in space are so great that using miles to measure them is not convenient—the numbers are too big to handle easily. So *light-years* are used instead. A light-year is equal to the distance traveled by light in one year in a vacuum (that is, with nothing, not even dust particles, in its way to slow it down). It's equal to almost six trillion (6,000,000,000,000) miles.

Star Magnitude

Stars differ greatly in brightness, or *magnitude*. Keep this constantly in mind as you observe, because the fainter stars may often be blotted out completely by lights or haze. The charts indicate the magnitude of the stars by using these symbols:

| 0 and brighter | 1 | 2 | 3 | 4 | 5 and fainter |

The lower the magnitude, the brighter the star. Stars of zero and first magnitude are usually grouped together as first-magnitude stars. There are twenty-one of these in the entire sky, and they are the brightest. You can't miss seeing them as soon as you go out at night.

The second-magnitude stars number about fifty (the Polestar is one of them). The third-magnitude stars are fairly bright, and there are about 150 of them. All the first-, second-, and third-magnitude stars appear on our charts, as well as more than 600 fourth-magnitude stars, which are fainter but still visible on clear nights.

Fifth-magnitude stars are, for the most part, the dimmest you can see under good conditions. There are about 1500 of them, but less than a hundred are shown on these charts. We include the ones that join brighter stars to make a distinctive shape, and so are more visible by their grouping. No sixth-magnitude stars appear on the charts—you have to have a clear night and excellent vision, a telescope, or field glasses to see them.

Star Color

At first glance all stars seem to be white, but once you begin watching individual stars carefully, you may be surprised to find they have different colors. Some have a bluish tint, some are reddish, some yellowish, some orangish, and some even greenish. The coloring is faint, but it's there.

Because star colors tell about their physical condition and temperature, they give useful information to the scientist. For us, however, they will simply be another way to distinguish between them as we watch—another element of God's creativity to enjoy.

The Whole Sky Charts

In addition to the seventeen biblical constellation charts in this book, you'll find at the end of the book a series of twelve *whole sky charts*. They will help you find a constellation during a particular time of year.

Study a constellation first in the chart in this section, along with the Bible story and historical or scientific facts

about its stars. This will get you acquainted with what to look for. Once you're familiar with the constellation, use the whole sky charts to find out when it appears and where.

The whole sky charts will tell you what the sky looks like from month to month. They are geared to the latitude 40° north (close to the latitude of Philadelphia, Pennsylvania; Springfield, Illinois; and Denver, Colorado). How the sky looks to *you* will depend upon how far north or south you are from that latitude. (Some constellations will appear higher or lower in the sky.)

We must use more than one chart because the sky is constantly changing as the stars move around the pole. If you watch the sky on and off for a few hours on the same evening, you'll see the difference. Stars that were in the west a few hours ago are gone below the horizon now; stars that were high in the sky are lower now in the west; stars that were low in the east are higher now; and new stars have come up over the eastern horizon.

At the same time, the sky changes across the seasons. The turning of the stars around the pole takes four minutes less than a full day. So each day the stars rise four minutes earlier than the day before. Those four minutes add up as we move through the year; one month from now, the stars will rise two hours earlier than they did today. Two hours a month equals twenty-four hours a year. After a year the whole cycle will repeat itself.

If you're ready now, turn to the next section to begin locating a book full of Bible stories in the sky.

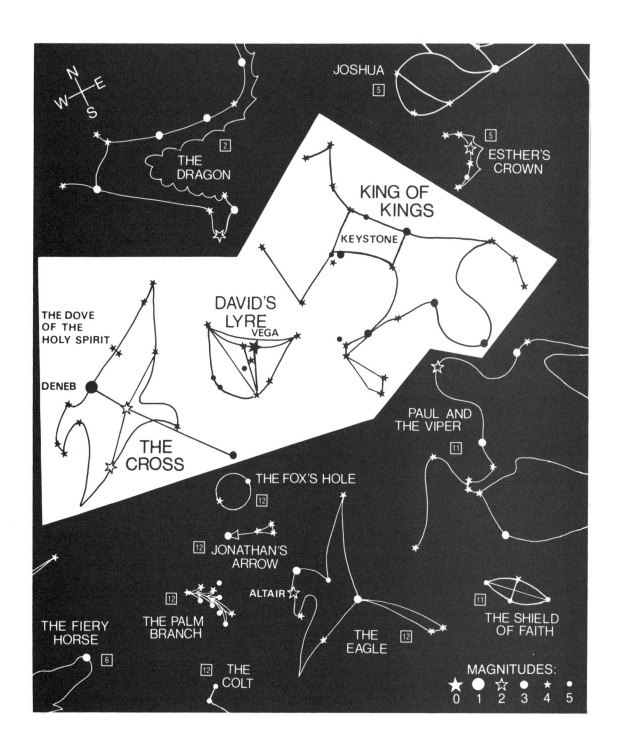

CONSTELLATION CHART 1

THE BIBLICAL CONSTELLATION CHARTS

THE CROSS: Of all the constellations in the sky, perhaps the most meaningful is one that forms the Cross. It's fitting that we should learn this group first, as a reminder that Jesus Christ is worthy to be first in our lives. Seven stars form the Cross, which reminds us as well of the seven stars Jesus held in his hand when John saw him in a vision (Revelation 1:13-16).

To find the Cross, you can start at the Big Dipper (see page 32 if you need help finding the Big Dipper). Just draw a line in your imagination through the two stars of the Dipper's bowl near the handle. Then let the line keep going beyond the lip of the bowl, far across the sky. It will run right into the top star in the Cross, which lies in the middle of the Milky Way.

Many ancient peoples saw this group of seven stars, plus a few more nearby, as some kind of bird—most commonly an eagle, a hen, or a swan. From the chart, you can see why this shape was imagined to be flying: Connecting the stars out beyond the arms of the Cross makes a pattern that looks like wings. For that reason, we can imagine a bird here, with its wings outstretched over the Cross. The bird, of course, is the dove of the Holy Spirit.

There are many places in the Bible where you can read about the Cross, and what it means to Christians. One good place to start, however, is in Colossians 1:13-20, where the apostle Paul tells us about why Jesus came and how he made peace with God for us by shedding his blood on the Cross. Some other important Scriptures to read are Colossians 2:13-15; Galatians 6:14; and Luke 9:23-25.

There are also many places where you can read about the Holy Spirit. To find out why we picture him as a dove, see Matthew 3:16, 17. Of course, the Spirit is not always as gentle as this little bird; Acts 2:1-4 will tell you why we sometimes picture him as fire, too. You can also read about the Holy Spirit in John 14:15-19; II Corinthians 3:17, 18; and Galatians 5:22-25.

An interesting star in the Cross, the one at its very top, is called *Deneb*. This white star can be seen at some time any night of the year. Deneb is 10,000 times more luminous than our sun, but it's so far away, it appears to us only as a bright speck. Sometime when you have binoculars handy, take a look around this region of the sky. It's full of many other beautiful stars of various colors.

Official constellation name: Cygnus, the Swan.

DAVID'S LYRE: David's Lyre is a small constellation, near the right arm of the Cross. Lyres are stringed musical instruments, similar to harps, which were used in Bible times. King David played the lyre, as did the Levites at the Temple, where there were always at least nine ready for worship. Lyres had anywhere from three to twelve strings, so we'll imagine this constellation with three.

The ancient Hebrews considered the lyre the most noble instrument of all, and the Bible tells of many times when it was used to praise God. So this constellation can be a symbol of worship for us, which is the lyre's traditional meaning. Since it appears right beside the Cross, it can remind us especially to praise God for his Son.

To get an idea of how David and others used lyres in the Bible to worship, read II Samuel 6:1-5; II Chronicles 5; Psalm 57:8; and Psalm 150. (In some translations, the word "harp" may be used instead of "lyre.")

The star pattern we call David's Lyre was imagined by different ancient peoples to be a harp, a cymbal, a fiddle, an eagle, a vulture, a goose, and even a turtle. One Christian astronomer of the past agreed with us that it was David's Lyre, but another said it was the manger in which the baby Jesus was laid.

The Lyre's brightest star, *Vega*, is the fifth brightest in the sky, and like Deneb can be seen at some time any night of the year. This brilliant blue-white star is actually a rather close neighbor of ours, as stars go—only 23 light-years away. (Deneb is over 1000 light-years away.) In 1850, Vega became the first star ever to be photographed.

Official name: Lyra, the Lyre.

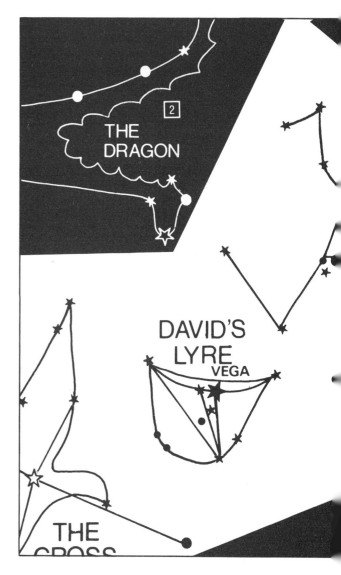

THE KING OF KINGS: Near the side of the Lyre opposite the Cross, find four stars that make a shape almost like a square. This shape has been called the *keystone*, because it looks like the top stone in the arch of a building. I Peter 2:6, 7 says that Jesus Christ is the *capstone* or top stone of God's House—his Church—because he's at its head. (Some translations say "cornerstone," meaning the top stone at the corner.)

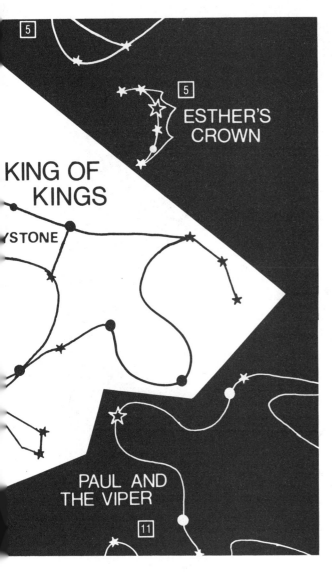

fighting with a sword. We find this Warrior in the Book of Revelation, where John wrote down a vision he had of Jesus coming back again to rule as King of the world.

In his vision, John saw the Lord Jesus at the head of a great army. He had a sword coming out of his mouth (in the constellation, he has taken it into his hand), and on his robe was written the name "King of Kings and Lord of Lords." You can read about this glorious day when Jesus comes back in Revelation 19:11-16. (If you find this book of the Bible a little hard to understand, however, don't worry; most people do!)

The star pattern forming the King of Kings was recognized by many ancient peoples as the shape of a great man, and it was called by many names, most of them heroes. Some saw it as a wrestler, some as a dancer, some as a man with a club. Early Christian astronomers said it was either Samson, Adam, or the three Wise Men.

On very clear nights you may see, in between the two keystone stars that form the King's right hip, a faint, hazy star. Actually, it's not a single star, but a cluster of around 100,000 stars! If you're ever looking through a telescope, this is a beautiful sight to observe.

Official name: Hercules, the Strong Man.

BEST TIMES to see the Cross: June through November. David's Lyre: May through November. The King of Kings: May through October. Whole sky charts 1, 6-12.

So it shouldn't be surprising that these four stars form within this constellation part of a figure that pictures Jesus: the One who is our "keystone" in God's House, the Church.

The rest of the stars in this group are rather dim, but if you start with the keystone, you should be able to find them by using the chart. They form a large picture of a mighty Warrior

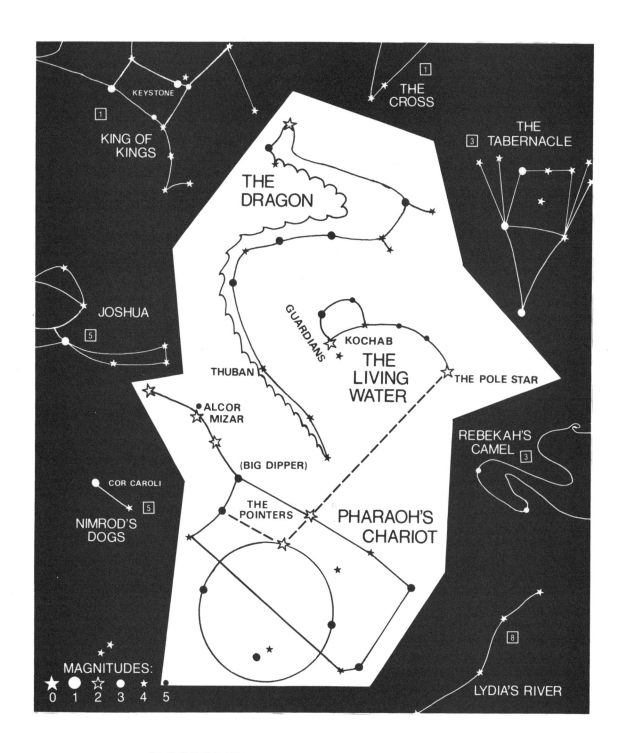

THE CROSS [1]

THE [3] TABERNACLE

KEYSTONE

KING OF KINGS [1]

THE DRAGON

JOSHUA [5]

GUARDIANS

KOCHAB

THE LIVING WATER

THE POLE STAR

THUBAN

REBEKAH'S CAMEL [3]

ALCOR
MIZAR

(BIG DIPPER)

COR CAROLI

NIMROD'S DOGS [5]

THE POINTERS

PHARAOH'S CHARIOT

[8]

MAGNITUDES:

0 1 2 3 4 5

LYDIA'S RIVER

CONSTELLATION CHART 2

THE DRAGON: If you look just beneath the left heel of the King of Kings, you'll see stars that form a pointy head attached to a long, curvy body. Almost every ancient people, including the Hebrews, claimed that this constellation looks like a wicked, slithering dragon. (You can also locate this group by starting from the Polestar, which is at the tip of the "handle" of the star group commonly known as the Little Dipper. The Dragon's body winds around the Little Dipper.)

In Revelation 12:7-10, Satan is described as a dragon who makes war against Heaven. So this constellation represents that old dragon, Satan. But why, you might ask, would we want a picture of our enemy in the stars?

The answer is simple. Look again at the chart: The King of Kings, Jesus, has his foot above the head of the Dragon, which was what ancient kings did to their enemies when they conquered them in battle. These two constellations remind us, then, that the Devil loses when he fights against Jesus.

The stars form a picture of what God had said would happen, long ago in the Garden of Eden (Genesis 3). The Devil had taken the shape of a serpent or snake, which is much like a dragon, and he had lied to Eve. So the Lord told Satan that a man would someday crush that serpent head beneath his heel—that is, he would defeat the Devil in battle. Jesus fulfilled that promise when he defeated Satan at the Cross. Now the King of Kings and the Dragon in the sky illustrate that victory.

But there's another way as well that we can picture God's defeat of Satan. Remember how we said in an earlier chapter that the stars seem to move across the sky because the earth is turning? Actually, there's also a second type of movement of the earth, much slower than the spinning. You may be surprised to find out that the earth wobbles a little as it turns, making the position of the stars in the sky change very gradually over thousands of years.

Though the Polestar is the "center" of our turning night sky now, it hasn't always been. Because of the earth's wobble, we once pointed in a slightly different direction, so that one of the stars in the Dragon's tail (*Thuban*) was the Polestar, with all the other stars turning around it. (This was quite long ago—during the earliest Old Testament times.) This means that the Dragon was once at the "center" of the sky, the place which some ancient peoples thought to be a position of authority.

Very slowly, however, the Dragon has been "cast down" from that place. He no longer possesses the Polestar, and he is sinking lower and lower in the sky. It's as if the Dragon constellation is telling the story from Revelation 12:7-9 about how Satan has been cast down from his place in Heaven. So it's a useful reminder to us of that truth.

Official name: Draco, the Dragon.

THE LIVING WATER: The Polestar is in one of the best-known star groups, commonly called the Little Dipper. Polaris forms the tip of the Dipper's "handle," which leads up to a small bowl at the end.

Because a dipper is used to get water, this constellation reminds us of the woman at the well who drew water for Jesus to drink on a hot day. As they talked, Jesus told her of some water he could give her that would keep her from ever getting thirsty again. To find out what this "living water" was, read what happened that day, in John 4:1-26.

This constellation has also been thought to look like many different figures besides a dipper: a bear, a dog's tail, a jackal, a string of jewels, a fish, a chariot, a bugle, and a leopard, to name a few. Some have included it as a part of the nearby Dragon, saying that it shows his wings. Christian astronomers of the past saw here the chariot Joseph sent to bring his father down to Egypt, or the bear that David killed. Whatever name was given to it, the Living Water has always been an important group because it contains the Polestar.

Most of the stars in this constellation are faint. Only the two at the end of the bowl are fairly bright. They are called the Guardians of the Pole, because they march around the Polestar like guards. The brighter of these two stars, Kochab (at the top right corner of the Dipper's bowl), was the Polestar about the time of Nehemiah (the fifth century before Christ).

Official name: Ursa Minor, the Little Bear.

PHARAOH'S CHARIOT: Surrounding the Big Dipper is a very large constellation that several ancient peoples thought resembled a chariot or

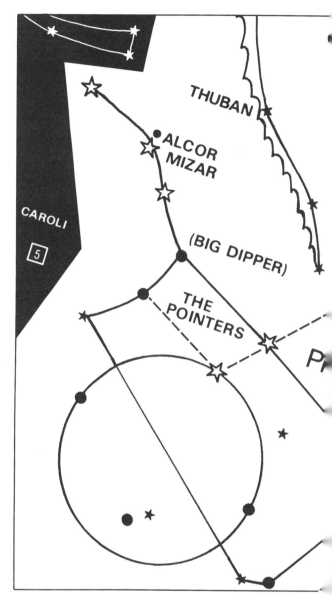

wagon. To trace its pattern, find the Big Dipper first, whose handle forms the horses' reigns. (The horses themselves don't appear.) Then draw an imaginary circle for the wheel, beginning with the star at the bottom right corner of the Dipper's bowl, and moving around through several of the brighter stars nearby.

46

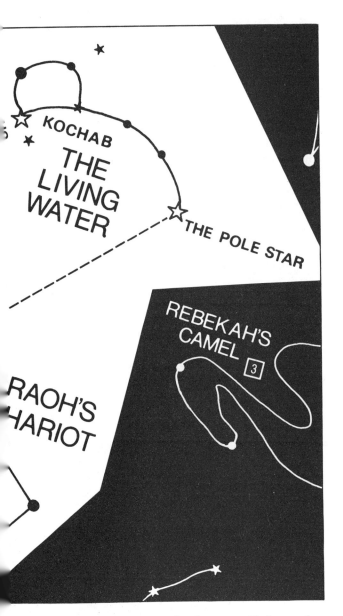

KOCHAB

THE LIVING WATER

THE POLE STAR

REBEKAH'S CAMEL ③

RAOH'S HARIOT

As the people were trying to leave the country, Pharaoh chased them in his own chariot, along with more than six hundred other chariots and officers of his army. When the Israelites came to the edge of the Red Sea, the Egyptians thought they had them trapped—but God had a few surprises in store. To find out what happened, read the story in Exodus 14:

Pharaoh's Chariot is probably the best known of all the star groups, and has had many other names around the world. The mention of constellations in Job 9:9 includes a word that Bible scholars believe refers to this star group. Most Bible versions translate it as "the Bear," which is what the Hebrews called the stars around the Big Dipper.

Many other ancient peoples also thought it looked like a bear—not only in Europe and Asia, but in North America as well. Yet this is puzzling, because the Dipper's handle was considered to form the bear's long tail, and bears don't *have* long tails! The Native Americans, however, were more realistic: They said the three bright stars of the Dipper's handle were not a tail, but rather three hunters chasing the bear. The faint star next to the bright middle star was a pot to cook him in.

Horse-drawn chariots, a swift form of transportation in biblical times, are mentioned throughout Scripture. They usually appear in war stories, because chariots were often used in battle. One well-known Bible story with chariots tells how Moses and the Israelites escaped from Pharaoh, who wanted to keep them in slavery in Egypt.

Other names for the Chariot are fascinating: the Wild Boar, the Reindeer, the Butcher's Cleaver, the Plough, the Bull's Thigh, the Brood Hen, even the Casserole! In the past, Christian star watchers have also nicknamed it Elijah's Chariot, the Heavenly Wagon, St. Peter's Ship, and Lazarus's Coffin.

Several of the stars in Pharaoh's Chariot have interesting histories. Close to the middle one of the three stars (Mizar) in the reigns lies a tiny star, Alcor, which is faint but famous. Long ago, Alcor served as an eye test: If you could see it, your vision was good. It even gave rise to a popular saying about people who paid attention to details but missed the big picture: "He can see Alcor, but not the full moon."

Alcor was known long ago in Germany as Hans the Thumbkin. According to an old legend, Hans, a wagon driver, gave Jesus a lift when he was tired. When Hans was told he could have a wish granted as a reward, he chose to drive his wagon from east to west through all eternity. So here he sits on the highest of the horses in his heavenly team. (The story's not true, of course, but it's fun!)

Another old story is even stranger. The ancient peoples of northern Europe said that one of the big toes on the Giant (another constellation we'll look at later) froze and broke off. Then someone threw it at the middle horse of the wagon, where it still lies!

Mizar and Alcor have been commonly known in England as the Horse and Rider, with Mizar the horse and Alcor the rider. This is a fitting name for stars in Pharaoh's Chariot. (See Exodus 15:1, which is the first verse of a song Moses sang just after Pharaoh's chase to the Red Sea.)

Official Name: Ursa Major, the Great Bear.

BEST TIMES to see the Dragon: late May to early November. The Living Water: any time of year. Pharaoh's Chariot: February through June. Whole sky charts 7-11 for the Dragon; all charts for the Living Water and Pharaoh's Chariot.

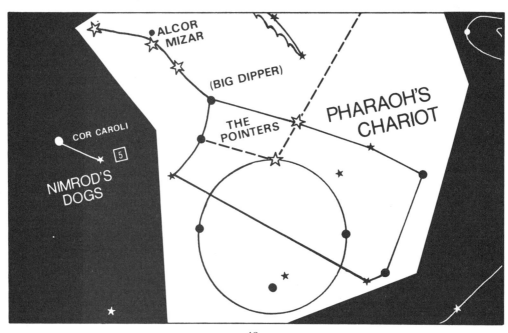

THE STORMY SEA: In your imagination, draw a line starting at the star in the Big Dipper where the handle joins the bowl, and running through the Polestar and beyond. It will soon run into a group of five bright stars that are well known because their shape is easy to remember. They form an almost perfect letter "W" (or an "M," of course, depending on its position).

Let the *W* stand for waves and the *M* for marine, and you'll see right away why we call this constellation the Stormy Sea. In fact, the similarity between the *M* shape and waves is no coincidence. The ancient Egyptian symbol from which our letter *M* developed stood for water, and was drawn to look like waves of the sea.

The Sea of Galilee was the setting of many events in the life of Jesus and his disciples. The weather in this area is often hard to predict, and a storm may form rather quickly. When it does, those who are in boats may be caught off guard.

This happened to the disciples one day. Imagine yourself in their place: The strong winds and high waves are making you fear for your lives, because the water is sweeping into the boat. It looks as if you'll sink any minute, and the water is too rough to swim. Meanwhile, Jesus is sleeping right through the storm!

What would you have done? To find out what happened, read Matthew 8:23-27. Another good story about a choppy sea—and two men walking on top of it!—is in Matthew 14:24-33.

The stars forming the Stormy Sea were recognized as a group very early in history. Pictures of it appear on four-thousand-year-old clay seals which were found in the valley of the Euphrates River. (This is the river which ran beside Abraham's birthplace, the city of Ur.)

Since that time, the constellation has been called by many names: the Woman of the Chair, the Key, the

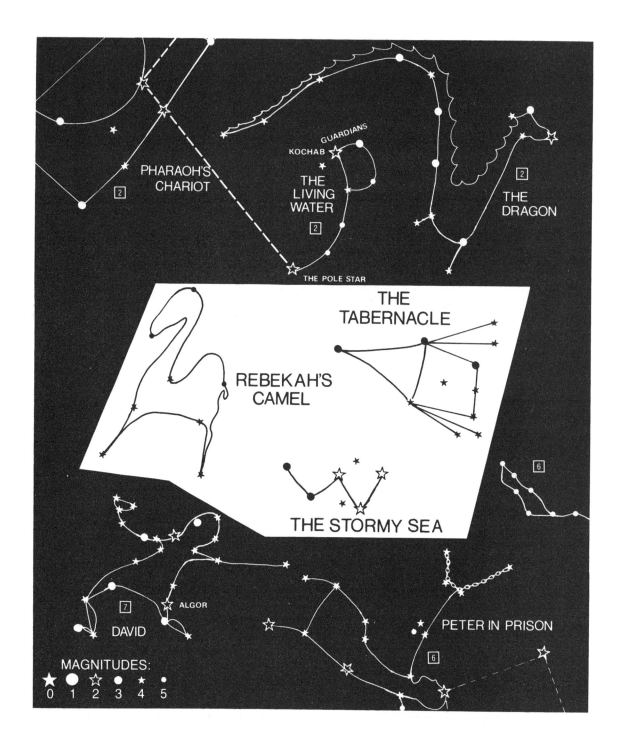

PHARAOH'S CHARIOT

2

THE LIVING WATER

KOCHAB GUARDIANS

2

THE POLE STAR

THE DRAGON

2

THE TABERNACLE

REBEKAH'S CAMEL

THE STORMY SEA

6

DAVID

7

ALGOR

PETER IN PRISON

6

MAGNITUDES:

★	●	☆	●	★	•
0	1	2	3	4	5

CONSTELLATION CHART 3

Hand, the Deer, the Kneeling Camel, the Girdle, and the Leg. Since the traditional Greek picture was of a Queen on her throne, Christian astronomers in the past associated it with Deborah, the woman judge of ancient Israel, or Bath-sheba, the royal mother of King Solomon. But it's difficult to see how this small pattern of five stars looks much like a woman, or even a throne.

In November of 1572, one of the most important events in the history of astronomy took place: A "new star" appeared in this constellation. Actually, this "new" star was probably a very old star which exploded, forming what is called a supernova. For a while it was brighter than the planet Venus.

At the time this supernova appeared, people had long been arguing about whether the heavens changed or always stayed the same. This supernova helped prove that the universe does change. It also created a great stir in its time among Christians: some thought it was another appearance of the Star of Bethlehem, and a sign that Christ's second coming was at hand.
Official name: Cassiopeia, the Queen.

THE TABERNACLE: If you continue the imaginary line from the Pointers in the Big Dipper past the Polestar, you'll run into stars that form a five-sided figure with a pointed top. It looks much like a tent, with a few stars around the bottom that can be imagined as tent pegs. (Whoever put the pegs down didn't arrange them very carefully, but the tent's still standing.) These stars are rather faint, so you must look carefully.

Because this group reminds us of a tent, we'll call it the Tabernacle. The tabernacle was a special tent which the Israelites carried around with them as they traveled through the wilderness on their way to the Promised Land. Inside the tabernacle, they kept the Ark of the Covenant, a chest containing the Ten Commandments on stone tablets. (The star in the middle of this constellation can be the Ark.)

The tabernacle was also called the Tent of Meeting, because that's where God often met with Moses and the people to speak to them. In a way, the tabernacle was like a portable church building, where people came to worship and to hear the Word of God.

The Bible gives a very thorough account of how the Lord wanted this tent to be built, and it runs for many chapters in the Book of Exodus. You can read the first part of this description in Exodus 25:1-22. Some other passages telling about the tabernacle are found in Exodus 33; 40:34-38; and Hebrews 9.

The stars which form the Tabernacle have been called the King (though the pattern looks very little like a man), the Fold (of sheep), and the Dog. Christian astronomers in the past labeled it either Stephen, the first Christian to die for the Lord, or King Solomon.
Official name: Cepheus, the King.

REBEKAH'S CAMEL: The handle of the Living Water dipper points roughly in the direction of Rebekah's Camel, a faint constellation that is hard to spot. In fact, its stars are of so little interest that it was not even considered a constellation until modern times.

The camel's neck is so long that it actually looks more like a giraffe, which is its official name. But Jakob Bartsch, the German astronomer who formed the constellation, said it was the camel that brought Rebekah to Isaac.

The account of Isaac and Rebekah's engagement is a beautiful story. You may not often picture camels as part of a romance (or giraffes, either, for that matter), but in this one camels play an important part. Find out how in Genesis 24.
Official name: Camelopardalis, the Giraffe.

BEST TIMES to see the Stormy Sea and the Tabernacle: August through January. Rebekah's Camel: November through March. Whole sky charts 1-12.

Keep in mind that the *best* viewing times are given here. These three constellations, along with Pharaoh's Chariot, the Dragon, and the Living Water, are *circumpolar*—that is, they are arranged around the Polestar and are not very far from it. For that reason, though they may be high or low in the sky as they travel around the Polestar, they're always above the horizon. They never rise or set, and can be seen any time of the year. (In the extreme southern parts of the United States, like Florida and Hawaii, they do dip partly below the horizon when they're low in the sky.)

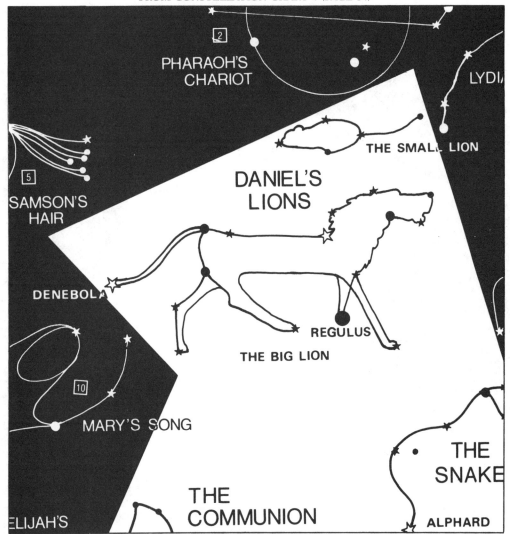

PHARAOH'S
CHARIOT

2

LYDI

THE SMALL LION

DANIEL'S
LIONS

5

SAMSON'S
HAIR

DENEBOLA

REGULUS

THE BIG LION

10

MARY'S SONG

THE
SNAKE

THE
COMMUNION

ELIJAH'S

ALPHARD

DANIEL'S LIONS: The prophet Daniel was a wise and brave man, and he did many deeds that made people remember him. But even if we knew nothing about his life except that he spent the night in a lions' den—and lived to tell the story—Daniel would probably still be well remembered for his courage (see Daniel 6). In the sky we find a big lion and a little one next to each other, so they seem a natural to be called Daniel's Lions, and we can

picture them as the hungry cats who were expecting Daniel for supper.

The big Lion is a large constellation with three bright stars. The brightest one, *Regulus*, is easy to find when the Big Dipper is high up. Draw a straight line between the two stars of the bowl next to the handle, continuing it past the wheel of Pharaoh's Chariot. It will hit the first star in the Lion's shoulder and then Regulus, which is at the end

53

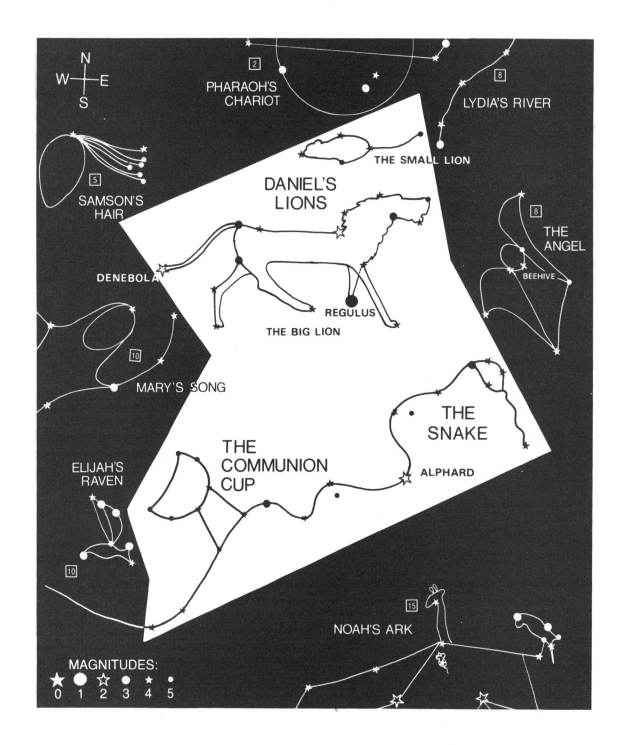

CONSTELLATION CHART 4

of the Lion's right forepaw. The Lion's front part is known as the *Sickle.* You could also call it a backwards question mark, with Regulus as the dot.

The second Lion is very faint, just above the big Lion's head. Actually, it's so small that no one paid it much attention until a few centuries ago. Its stars form a diamond shape with a tail, so you can imagine it as a tiny cub curled up asleep.

Even so, it looks more like a mouse. If you can believe that a mouse would dare to be seen in a lions' den, feel free to imagine it as one. He could be scampering across the wall out of paw's reach.

The story of Daniel's night with the lions is a familiar one to most folks. But if you ever find you need a little extra faith in God's care for you (and most of us do), try reading it again in Daniel 6.

The Lion also has special meaning as a symbol for Jesus. When Jacob blessed his sons before he died, he said that Judah would be like a mighty lion who rules (Genesis 49:9). So the lion became the symbol of Judah's tribe. Since Jesus was of the tribe of Judah, the Book of Revelation calls him "the Lion of the tribe of Judah" (Revelation 5:5), the One who will rule the world. This constellation, then, can remind us of the Lord's kingship.

In the traditional scheme, these two figures form separate constellations, the Lion and the Little Lion. The smaller one was only created in modern times. But the bigger group is one of the oldest constellations, and it was known as a lion to the Hebrews. In fact, the ancient Greeks, Turks, Persians, Syrians, and Babylonians all agreed that it was a big cat. But the Chinese thought it was a horse.

Others made a picture from just the front part, which they called the Curved Weapon, the Scimitar (a curved sword), or the Forehead. Early Christian star watchers agreed with us that it was Daniel's lion.

Regulus is a blue-white star of first magnitude, about twice as bright as the Polestar. It's around 80 light-years away, and is over 100 times more luminous than the sun. Regulus means "little king," and the title of royalty was given to it by many ancient peoples. *Denebola* is the name of the bright star at the end of the big Lion's tail.

The larger Lion is in the *zodiac,* which is a belt of twelve constellations across the sky. Zodiac means "animal belt," because all the constellations in it originally were pictures of animals. The sun, moon, and planets all travel across the sky within this area, so you can expect sometimes to see one or more "wanderers" in the Lion. (For a list of constellations in the Zodiac, see the appendix in the back of this book.)

Along the middle of the zodiac runs the *ecliptic.* This is an imaginary line drawn along the path the sun travels through the heavens during a year's time. Regulus is almost exactly on the ecliptic. The moon crosses the ecliptic at regular times, so it may sometimes hide Regulus.

Official names: Leo, the Lion: Leo Minor, the Little Lion.

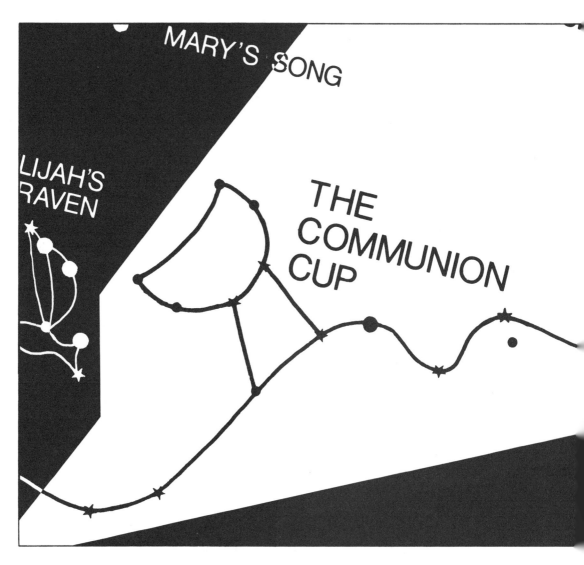

MARY'S SONG

ELIJAH'S RAVEN

THE COMMUNION CUP

THE SNAKE: The largest constellation in our skies is so long that it doesn't fit into any one chart (the tail will be found on chart 10). The Snake, as it's called, is not very bright. It has a single star of second magnitude, *Alphard*, that only looks bright because it has no nearby competition.

To find the Snake, look first for the head: Draw an imaginary line through the two stars which form the big Lion's forepaws. If you continue this line away from the Lion's body, it will hit the Snake's head. The tail wanders off from there across a quarter of the sky.

The Snake, of course, is the shape Satan took in the Garden of Eden, when he wanted to tempt Eve into eating from the forbidden tree. To read about how he tricked her into disobeying God, read Genesis 3:1-7. Later, we'll take up the story from

56

THE SNAKE

ALPHARD

THE COMMUNION CUP: About halfway down the back of the Snake sits a group of stars shaped like a chalice or cup. This constellation, the Communion Cup, is small and rather faint. In the middle latitudes, it's hard to see. But further south, where it rises higher, the cup shape can be traced easily on a dark, clear night.

The Cup brings to mind the Last Supper Jesus ate with his disciples before he died and was raised again. As a symbol of Holy Communion, it reminds us of the blood he shed for our sakes. It also is a sign of our fellowship with other believers, because Christians everywhere take part in Communion as a way of remembering the Lord. To read about Jesus' Last Supper, see Matthew 26:17-30. The apostle Paul also has some important words to say about it in I Corinthians 10:16, 17.

Several ancient peoples saw this figure as a bowl or cup, including the Jews. A few centuries ago, the English called it a Two-Handed Pot. Christian astronomers in the past said it was a picture of Joseph's Cup (placed in Benjamin's sack), the Wine Cup of Noah, the Water Jars in Cana, or the Communion Cup. One of them combined it with a few other stars to make the Ark of the Covenant.

Official name: Crater, the Cup.

there with another constellation, the Flaming Sword (which, by the way, appears in the sky with Adam and Eve not far from the Snake).

Ancient peoples gave this constellation several names: the Water Snake; the Dragon; the Ax; and the Nile River. Early Christian astronomers called it the Jordan River or the Flood.

Official name: Hydra, the Water Snake.

BEST TIMES to see Daniel's Lions: February through June. The Snake (at least its head): February through May. The Communion Cup: April and May. Whole sky charts 3-7.

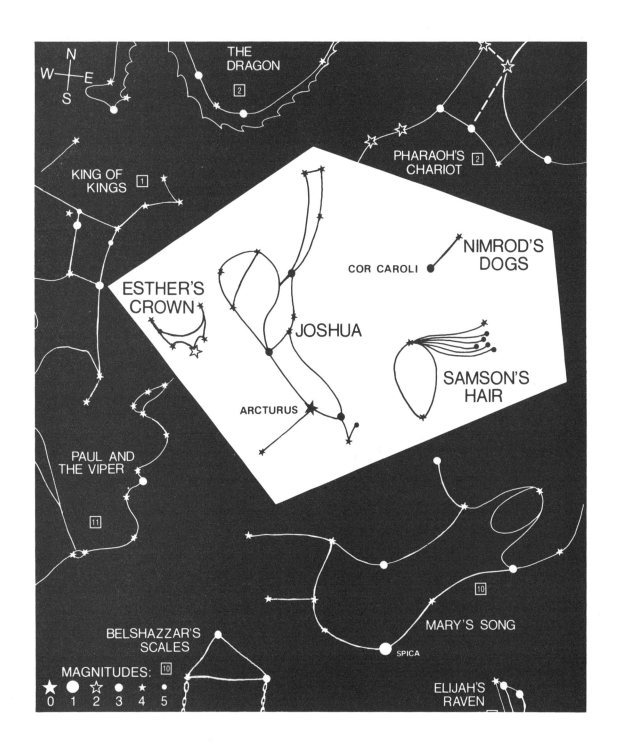

CONSTELLATION CHART 5

JOSHUA: If you follow the sweep of the Big Dipper's handle, away from the bowl, you'll run into the fourth brightest star in the heavens, orange *Arcturus*. Arcturus is the main star in one of the oldest recorded constellations, which we'll call Joshua. To trace the rest of the picture, try to find the triangle of stars that form his helmet first. Next locate the large head, the ram's horn trumpet in his mouth, and finally his short legs. The horn and the legs are rather faint, so it takes a clear night to see them.

We've all heard how Joshua fought the battle of Jericho, and the walls came tumbling down. The amazing part of this story, of course, is how Jericho was conquered without even a fight. The ram's horn you see in this constellation is a reminder of the miracle God worked for the army of Israel. You can read about it in Joshua 5:13—6:20.

This constellation was called by the ancient Hebrews the Barking Dog. Others saw it as a wolf, a wagon driver, a herdsman, a shepherd, or a bear keeper. One Christian astronomer thought it should be the prophet Amos, who was also a shepherd. If you look only at the brighter stars, you could also say it looks much like a kite or an ice-cream cone.

Arcturus has been admired and written about from earliest times, and was probably one of the first stars to be named. It's a giant star, about 25 times the diameter of our sun, and is 100 times as luminous. It's also a rather close neighbor, only forty light-years away. In late spring and early summer, Arcturus is the first star you see after sunset, shining high up in the sky. Perhaps its greatest claim to fame in recent times is that it opened the Chicago World's Fair in 1934—by shining on a photoelectric cell!
Official name: Bootes, the Herdsman.

NIMROD'S DOGS: Just beneath the Big Dipper's handle is a pair of stars, one brighter than the other. The brighter one is known as *Cor Caroli*. This modern constellation was first called the Hunting Dogs, though it really has no animal shape.

Nimrod was an ancient king of Mesopotamia, "a mighty hunter before the Lord." So we've named these two stars Nimrod's Dogs, to show the hounds he might have used in hunting. We don't know much more about Nimrod, but he was evidently a famous and powerful ruler in his day. You can read about him in Genesis 10:8-10.
Official name: Canes Venatici, the Hunting Dogs.

ESTHER'S CROWN: The Big Dipper's handle points toward a second-magnitude star just beyond Joshua's head. Its name is *Gemma*, and it's the brightest jewel in a small but graceful half circle of stars called Esther's Crown.

Esther was a brave Jewish heroine of the Old Testament. Because of her great beauty, she was made queen, and because of her great courage, she saved the whole Jewish nation from destruction. You can read her story in the book that carries her name.

The ancient Hebrews, like the Greeks and others, agreed that this half circle

was a crown. Arabs considered it a dish or a bowl, while some Native Americans said it was a circle of dancing girls. Native Australians, meanwhile, were certain it was a boomerang! One Christian astronomer suggested that it was the Crown of Thorns.
Official name: Corona Borealis, the Northern Crown.

SAMSON'S HAIR: On the other side of Nimrod's Dogs from the Big Dipper is a small group of dim stars. They are visible only on a clear, moonless night, when the constellation is high up in the sky. When you draw an imaginary line between each of them and a slightly brighter star in the nearby east, the resulting picture suggests a shock of long hair. That's how most ancient peoples saw this constellation, so we have called it Samson's Hair.

Samson's famous long hair was a sign that he was a Nazirite, set apart for God since his birth. He was so strong he could tear a hungry lion apart with his bare hands. But Samson's weakness was in his heart—his feelings for a deceitful lady. Delilah double-crossed him, and the rest of his life was a sad story. To learn from Samson's mistake, read about him in Judges 16:4-31.

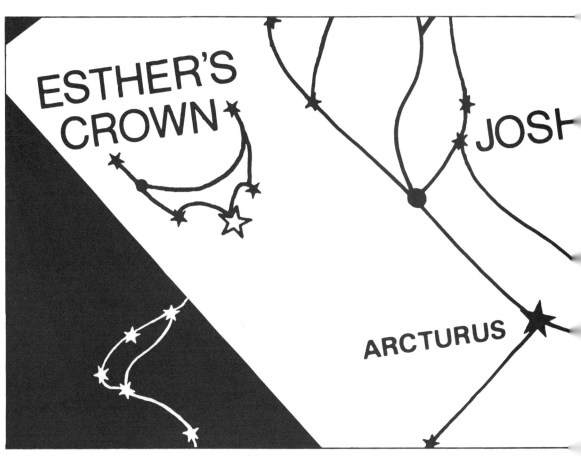

Other pictures for this cluster of stars have been a rose, a sheaf of wheat, an ivy wreath, and a pond. Some made it the tuft at the end of the big Lion's tail. Early Christian astronomers saw in the constellation the flagellum or whip used to lash Jesus before he was crucified.

These stars have also been called the Veil of Veronica. According to an old legend, Veronica was a woman of Jerusalem who wiped the blood off Jesus' face as he carried the cross to Calvary. An image of the Lord's face was supposed to have appeared on the veil by a miracle of God.

Of all our constellations, Samson's Hair is the farthest away from the band of the Milky Way. In this direction we can see beyond our own galaxy into great depths of space.
Official name: Coma Berenices, Berenice's Hair.

BEST TIMES to see Joshua, Esther's Crown, and Samson's Hair: April through August. Nimrod's Dogs: February through June. Whole sky charts 3-9 for Nimrod's Dogs, 4-9 for the others.

SAMSON'S HAIR

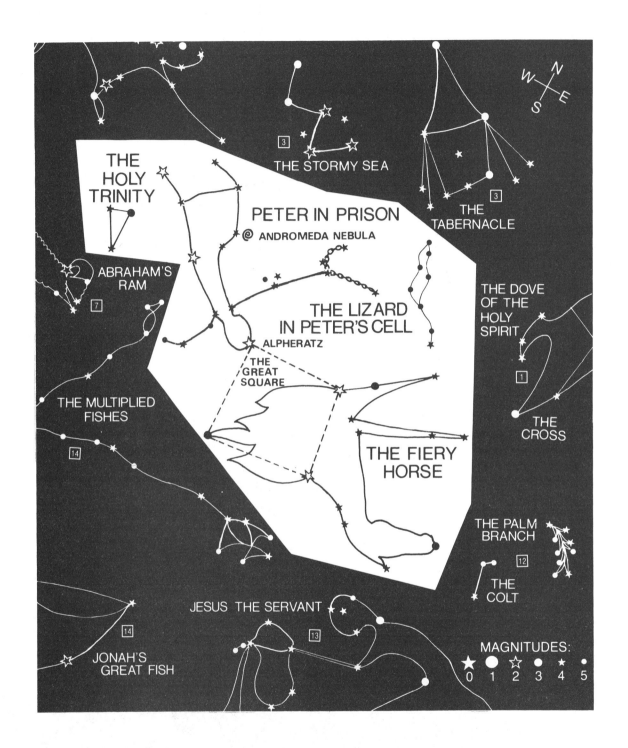

THE
HOLY
TRINITY

THE STORMY SEA

3

PETER IN PRISON

@ ANDROMEDA NEBULA

THE TABERNACLE

3

ABRAHAM'S
RAM

7

THE LIZARD
IN PETER'S CELL

ALPHERATZ

THE DOVE
OF THE
HOLY
SPIRIT

1

THE
GREAT
SQUARE

THE MULTIPLIED
FISHES

14

THE FIERY
HORSE

THE
CROSS

THE PALM
BRANCH

12

THE
COLT

JESUS THE SERVANT

13

JONAH'S
GREAT FISH

14

MAGNITUDES:

0 1 2 3 4 5

CONSTELLATION CHART 6

THE GREAT SQUARE: The Arabs called this figure the Water Bucket, but it's not usually thought of as a constellation in itself. Even so, the Great Square is one of the landmarks of the sky. Inside of its four corner stars is a rather blank space, with only a few very faint stars. Three of the Square's corners belong to the Fiery Horse, and the fourth belongs to Peter in Prison. The Great Square can help you find these two constellations.

To find the Square, draw a straight line from the Polestar through the first star in the *M* of the Stormy Sea, and on beyond. The line will pass diagonally across the Square, running through the star in Peter's head and the tip of the flame in the Fiery Horse. This shape is so striking that you'll never forget it once you learn it.

PETER IN PRISON: In our chart, Peter is standing on his head, which is one of the four stars of the Great Square. After you find his head, spot the three bright stars forming one side of his body and one leg. Then find the rest. The other leg is made up of dimmer stars.

The small curve of stars around Peter's right wrist are a chain, and you can imagine one on his left wrist as well. Peter is in prison for preaching the Gospel. He's waiting to stand trial before King Herod, who probably wants to kill him. But Herod didn't figure on Peter getting some unusual help. To find out how Peter escaped, read the amazing story in Acts 12:1-19.

Just beyond the chain on Peter's right wrist is a small, very faint group of stars in the Milky Way. In modern times this group has been made into a separate constellation called the Lizard, but it hardly seems worth an extra name. We'll consider it part of Peter's constellation. Since lizards were certain to be found crawling around an ancient prison cell, you can think of this star group as a little reptile creeping down the wall next to Peter's hand.

Peter in Prison has also been called a threshing floor, a seal (the animal), and a widow. One early Christian astronomer said it was Abigail, a wife of King David. Another named it the Tomb of Jesus.

The most common tradition, however, is that it pictures a woman chained to a rock. A very old legend, perhaps going back to the time of Abraham and before, tells how a princess was to be sacrificed to a sea monster as a punishment for her mother's pride. (She was rescued in the end by a brave hero.) Many cultures had this legend, in different forms.

The princess gave her name, Andromeda, to the most distant object the unaided human eye can see in the sky. Near Peter's right hip you can see a small hazy spot if the night is extremely clear and moonless. This is the famous *Andromeda Nebula*, a galaxy like our own Milky Way. It's made up of 100 billion stars, and is about 2.7 million *light-years* (not miles) away.

The bright star *Alpheratz* (Peter's head) has sometimes been grouped with this constellation, and other times with the Horse constellation above him (see below). If you put it with the horse,

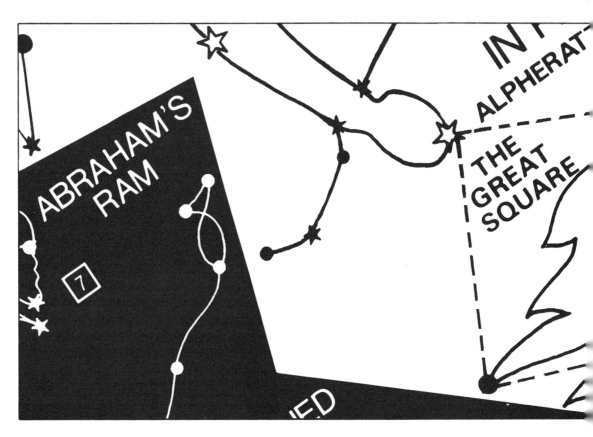

however, Peter is beheaded. Herod would be pleased, but that's not how the story ended.
Official names: Andromeda, the Woman Chained; Lacerta, the Lizard.

THE FIERY HORSE: You can trace this constellation from the other three corners of the Great Square. These stars form the tip of the flame and the two points where it joins the horse's body. Only the horse's front half can be seen; the rest is ablaze. The group isn't as bright as Peter in Prison, but you can trace it under good conditions.

A Fiery Horse sounds like a strange creature, and it is. Two of them appeared when it was time for Elijah to go to Heaven. They pulled a fiery chariot in a whirlwind that carried him away. Though this may seem an unusual way to go, Elijah was an unusual man, and he seemed to have a knack for drawing fire—both from Heaven and from the king. The story of his ride upward is in II Kings 2:1-18.

Most ancient cultures saw this star group as a horse; some added wings to the shoulders. One of its names from the Romans was "Noisy Footed." It might at one time have pictured the figurehead on a ship, which would explain why only half the horse appears in the traditional pictures.

Jewish legend called the constellation Nimrod's Horse. (In that case, his dogs have wandered far away from him

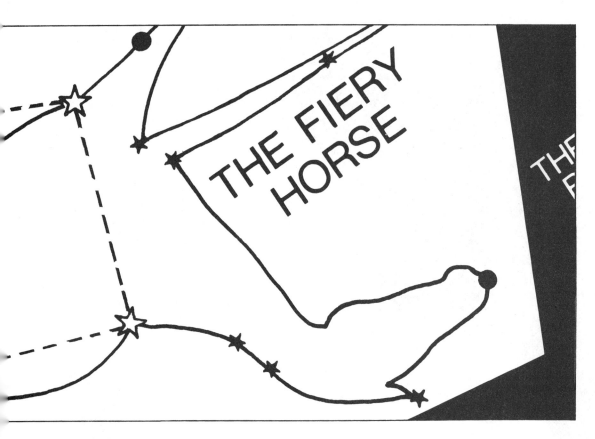

THE FIERY HORSE

THE F
P

across the sky.) Some Christians have called it the donkey Jesus rode into Jerusalem, while others said it was the angel Gabriel.
Official name: Pegasus, the Winged Horse.

THE HOLY TRINITY: Just off Peter's left foot is a tiny and faint triangle. The triangle is an ancient symbol of the Holy Trinity: God the Father, God the Son, and God the Holy Spirit. So it's natural that this constellation should have this title as a reminder of God's mysterious nature.

Christians long ago also noted that this triangle looks like the letter *delta* in the Greek alphabet, the language in which the New Testament was first written.

Because delta is the initial of the Greek word for God, this also was a meaningful connection.

The ancient Jews knew this group as the *Shalish*, which was a three-stringed instrument of triangular shape played in David's time. Other peoples saw it as the delta (triangular mouth) of the Nile River in Egypt; the island of Sicily, which is roughly a triangle; or a symbol of the three joined continents of Europe, Africa, and Asia.
Official name: Triangulum, the Triangle.

BEST TIMES to see Great Square: Aug. to Jan. Peter in Prison: September to January. Fiery Horse: August to October. Holy Trinity: October to January. Whole sky charts 1-3, 9-12.

65

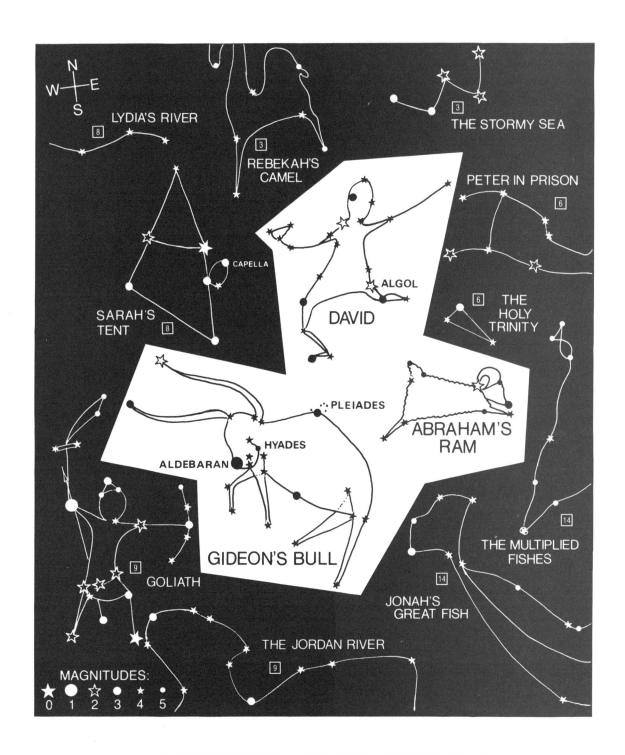

CONSTELLATION CHART 7

DAVID: Just below Peter's feet is a group of stars which has long been seen as a young hero of one sort or another. Imagine the star under Peter's right foot as a stone in the end of a sling, and this picture will fall in place. It's the shepherd boy David, of course, taking aim at Goliath. In David's other hand is the shepherd's pouch where he kept his five smooth stones.

Goliath is described in another chart. But it's easy to find him: Just follow the general direction the stone is aimed, past the head of Gideon's Bull.

The story of David and Goliath is one of the best known in the Bible, but it's always thrilling to read again. You can find it in I Samuel 17.

Some Christian astronomers of the past agreed with us that this constellation was David (though they pictured him already holding Goliath's head). Others said it was the apostle Paul with his book and the sword of the Spirit.

The bright star (second magnitude) in David's upper left leg is named *Algol*. Algol is a double star, or *binary*—that is, two stars rather close together, moving around each other. One star is bright; the other much darker. So when the dark star gets in front of the bright one (as seen from the earth), Algol grows dimmer.

A star that changes brightness in this way is called a *variable star*. You can watch the change in Algol if you're patient. Try looking at it on and off during each night for a few evenings in a row. You'll see why some have compared it to a winking eye.

Official name: Perseus, the Hero.

GIDEON'S BULL: Before David's stone can reach its mark on Goliath's forehead, it must pass between the horns of a great bull, whose shape has been recognized there from earliest times. Not only in Europe and the Near East, but even centuries ago in the Amazon Valley, people agreed: A beautiful cluster of stars was the animal's head, while two bright ones beyond were the tips of its long horns. It lies within the zodiac.

In biblical times, the bull was commonly offered as a sacrifice. One account in which such a sacrifice plays an important part is the story of Gideon. At the Lord's command, Gideon tore down the altar his father had built to a pagan God named Baal. Then he built a new altar to the Lord, and sacrificed one of his father's bulls on it.

Gideon was afraid that his family and the townspeople would be angry—they must have all worshiped Baal—so he went by night to follow God's instructions. The next morning, when they discovered what had happened, they searched until they found out who had done it. Then they decided to put Gideon to death. To find out what happened (and to learn how clever a dad can be), read this story in Judges 6:25-32.

Some Christians called this group of stars the apostle Andrew. Others said it was Joseph, the son of Israel who was sold into slavery.

The Bull is best known because of the *Pleiades*. This is a faint group of stars that looks at first glance like a small silver cloud on the Bull's back. If you look closer, however, you can find six individual little stars. (Only six are visible to the unaided eye today, though somehow most ancient star watchers saw seven.) People living in such widely scattered places as Germany, Rome, Africa, Arabia, and even Malaysia have all thought at some time or another that the Pleiades were the center of the universe.

This star cluster is a fascinating subject in itself. It's mentioned more often in poetry, stories, and history than any other group in the heavens. In fact, it's noted three times in the Bible, in Job 9:9 and 38:31, and in Amos 5:8.

Many titles have been given the Pleiades: the Razor, the Flame, the Bunch of Grapes, the Seven Doves, the Seven Sisters, the Flock, the Family, the Old Wives, the Sieve, the Mosquito Net, the Dog Pack, the Boar Pack, the Camel Herd, the Little Eyes, the Nanny Goats, the Dancers, and the Shovel. Late Jewish tradition called them the Hen with Her Chicks.

The Pleiades aren't the only special feature of Gideon's Bull. The cluster of stars forming the head are called the *Hyades*, yet another famous group. Both the Pleiades and the Hyades are star clusters traveling together through space.

The Hyades, too, have had many names: The "V," the Spoon, the Little Camels, the Little Pigs, the Temple, the Wagon, and the Boiling Sea. Any one of the three phrases in Job translated as "Bear," "chambers of the south," or "constellations" (9:9; 38:32) may refer to the Hyades, but we don't know for sure.

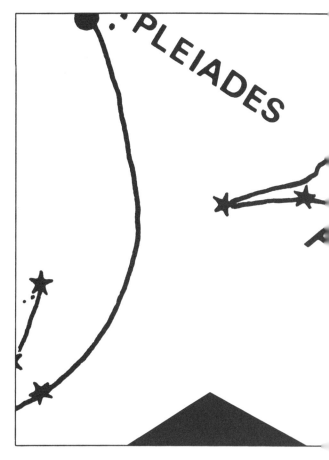

Once you find the Pleiades beneath David's right foot and the orange star (*Aldebaran*) at the Bull's nose, the rest of the constellation is easier to trace. *Aldebaran*, the Bull's brightest, is first-magnitude; it's thirty-six times the size of our sun, 100 times more luminous, and fifty-seven light-years away.

Official name: Taurus, the Bull.

ABRAHAM'S RAM: Halfway between the Pleiades and the Great Square is a faint constellation that wouldn't get much attention if it weren't in the zodiac. Look first for the two bright stars in its head. Then trace the rest of the shape to form Abraham's Ram.

THE HOLY TRINITY

ABRAHAM'S RAM

Like the bull, the ram (a grown male sheep) was in biblical times offered as a sacrifice to God. The sacrificial ram plays an important part in an Old Testament account of the life of Abraham. In this touching story, God tested Abraham to see if he was willing to obey him, even when he didn't understand the reasons for God's commands. The Lord told Abraham to sacrifice, not a bull or ram, but his own son, Isaac. That was a difficult command to obey, but Abraham loved God so much that he was willing to do it. The story has a happy ending, however (for everyone except the ram), and you can read it in Genesis 22:1-19.

Several ancient peoples saw in this constellation the shape of a ram or sheep, including the Hebrews. Early Christian astronomers said this group showed either Abraham's Ram, the Lamb of God (a name for Jesus), or the apostle Peter. In China, however, people saw here a dog. If you flatten the nose a little, it just might pass for a Pekingese.

Official name: Aries, the Ram.

BEST TIMES to see David: November through March. Gideon's Bull: October through March. Abraham's Ram: October through February. Whole sky charts 1-4, 11-12.

69

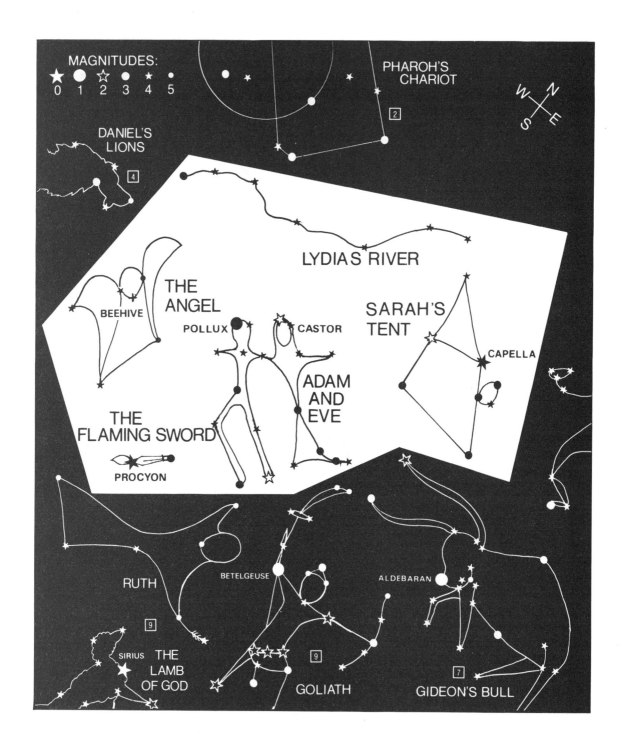

CONSTELLATION CHART 8

ADAM AND EVE: Starting at the star in the Big Dipper where the handle meets the bowl, draw a diagonal line across the bowl and far beyond. In the zodiac you'll run into a close pair of nearly identical bright stars. All around the world, from Europe to Babylonia to India to Polynesia, these two stars have been known as the heads of a human pair. The Hebrews and Greeks both called it the Twins; others said they were a brother and sister or a man and wife. We'll see it as the first and most famous couple in history, Adam and Eve.

Though the story of Adam and Eve's creation is familiar to most of us, we can always learn from hearing it again. You can read the story in Genesis 2.

Adam and Eve's heads are bright but the rest of their bodies are fainter, so you may need a clear night to trace the whole figure. They're holding hands and have stars in their eyes—good signs for a couple who have been married so long! In your imagination you can add fig leaves if you think Eve has already talked to the Snake, who's lurking nearby (just on the other side of Gabriel).

The two bright stars are named *Castor* and *Pollux*. Castor is white, a second-magnitude; Pollux is yellow, and a first-magnitude.

THE FLAMING SWORD: A broad, sweeping curve from the star Capella in Sarah's Tent (described below) through Castor and Pollux and on down takes you to one of the brightest stars in the sky, *Procyon*. It's a yellow-white, first-magnitude star that forms the fiery tip of the Flaming Sword of Eden. The hilt of the Sword is the dimmer star nearby.

When Adam and Eve were sent out of the Garden, God placed cherubim (a kind of angel) and the Flaming Sword on the east side of it to guard the way to the Tree of Life. So it makes sense that the Sword should appear next to the couple in the sky. To read about this sad event, see Genesis 4:23, 24.

Tradition has called this pair of stars a puppy, and one Christian astronomer said it was the Passover Lamb. But you can't make either of those shapes very easily with just two stars.

Procyon is one of our close neighbors, only ten and a half light-years away. It's five times as luminous as the sun, and is the eighth brightest star in our sky.
Official name: Canis Minor, the Little Dog.

THE ANGEL: Between the Flaming Sword and Daniel's Lions lies the faintest constellation in the zodiac. With its wings outstretched as if to fly, we'll call it the Angel.

The Angel's position is fitting: It stands near Adam and Eve and above the Flaming Sword, reminding us of the cherubim guarding the Tree of Life. Angels have taken part in many other events through history as well, but they are still a great mystery. We know very little about them.

To read about angels, you can choose from many stories. Gabriel is the angel who appears to Daniel and tells him about the future in Daniel chapters 10—12. He also mentions Michael here as a chief prince among angels (10:13, 21; 12:1). Gabriel is the one who announces to Mary that Jesus will be born, and to Zechariah that John the Baptist will be born. You can find those two events in the first chapter of Luke.

Another angel, Michael, also appears in Jude 9 and Revelation 12:7. In this last place, he is the one who leads the armies in victory over the Dragon, and casts him down from Heaven.

A number of other Bible stories talk about angels without giving their names. A few more to look at are Genesis 28:10-22; Judges 13; Matthew 2:1-21; and Luke 2:8-20.

The traditional picture here is a crab, which works with a little imagination. Others called it a lobster, a crayfish, a turtle, or a beetle. Christian astronomers long ago saw here either the Breastplate of Righteousness (Ephesians 6:14); the Manger of the Baby Jesus; or the writer of the fourth Gospel, John.

If the night is clear, you may be able to see a small, fuzzy patch on the Angel's chin. This is not a beard; rather, it's a cluster of stars known as the *Beehive*. You can see individual stars in it if you use binoculars. Other names for it in ancient times were the Little Cloud, the Crib, and the Stall. This last name was probably in honor of the two stars on either side of the Angel's head, known as the northern and southern donkeys.
Official name: Cancer, the Crab.

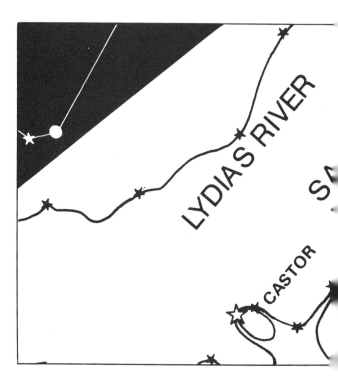

SARAH'S TENT: Extend the line along the top edge of the Big Dipper's bowl, moving away from the handle, and you'll run into a brilliant star of first magnitude, the sixth brightest in the sky. Named *Capella*, this yellow star lies near a trio of dimmer ones. The trio forms the head of Sarah, Abraham's wife. Capella is an upper corner of her tent, which is formed by five stars. So Sarah is sticking her head out of the tent's opening.

The Bible tells us that Sarah once stood at the entrance to her tent, listening in on a conversation between the Lord and her husband. She was frightened when the Lord caught her eavesdropping. Worse yet, she discovered that *he* had been listening to *her* conversation with herself. To find out what God said to Abraham and Sarah, read Genesis 18:1-15. Then,

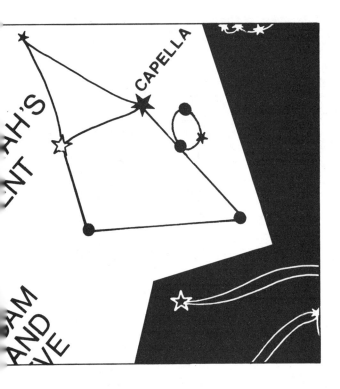

star nearest Capella, *Epsilon Aurigae*, is a double star whose size is 2700 times as great as the sun. It's the largest star we know about so far.
Official name: Auriga, the Charioteer.

LYDIA'S RIVER: Near the end of Pharaoh's Chariot, which is opposite the reigns, stretches a faint ribbon of stars. It's so dim that no one named it as a constellation until modern times, but it does look rather like a winding river. So we'll call it Lydia's River, after the one that ran by the place where the apostle Paul first met the woman by that name, outside the city of Philippi.

Lydia was called a worshiper of God, and that's a title every Christian would be honored to have. We know very little about her, except that her heart and home were both open to Paul. Lydia was a dealer in purple cloth, which was the fabric used by royalty. She may very well have been wealthy, then, and early Christian tradition claims she was quite generous. The Philippian church is said to have begun in her home. To read about how Paul and Lydia met, read Acts 16:11-15.

This constellation has been called the Lynx or Tiger, but at most it looks only like a lynx's back. The astronomer who named it admitted that the stars were so faint and few, you'd have to have a lynx's eyes to see them.
Official name: The Lynx.

so you don't end the story on a bad note, skip to chapter 21 and read the first six verses for a happier ending.

This constellation was traditionally the driver of a chariot (some said it was the lame king who invented the chariot). In one old drawing, he was pictured as driving a wagon behind a team made of two oxen, a horse, and a zebra! In other pictures, it's a shepherd holding a goat, with two kids (baby goats) nearby; a farmer at his plow; a mule; or a shepherd. Christians have in the past named it Jacob, or his son Joseph, or the Good Shepherd (Jesus).

Capella, who is the goat in the shepherd pictures, is sixteen times the size of the sun and 150 times as luminous. It's forty-two light-years away. Capella can be seen, for a short time at least, any night of the year. The

BEST TIMES to see Adam and Eve and the Flaming Sword: December through May. The Angel and Lydia's River: January through May. Sarah's Tent: October through April. Whole sky charts 1-6, 12.

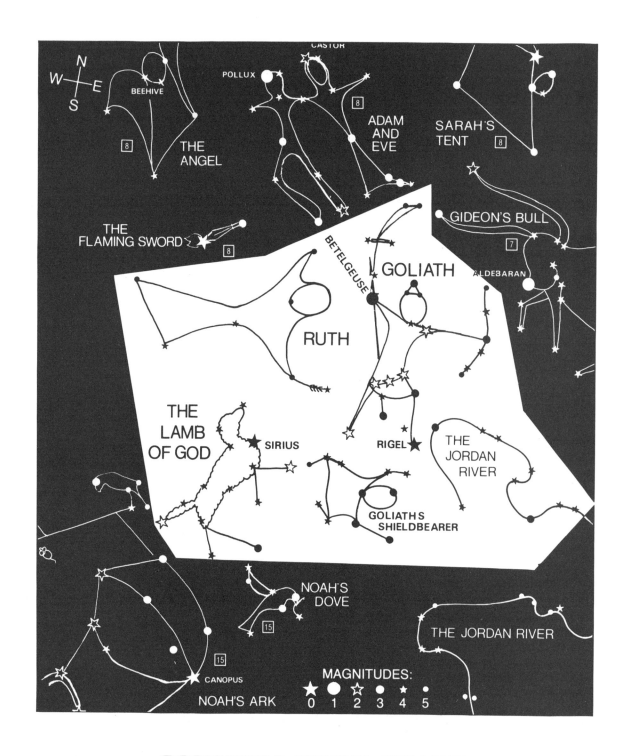

CONSTELLATION CHART 9

GOLIATH: Follow the path which the stone in David's sling would take (dropping down a little to allow for gravity). On beyond the horns of Gideon's Bull you should be able to find a brilliant star of first magnitude. Its name is *Betelgeuse.* Betelgeuse forms the right shoulder of Goliath, the giant David defeated with his sling. Near Betelgeuse is a striking row of three bright stars, all second magnitude. These form the bottom edge of Goliath's coat of mail. The rest of the figure should be easy to trace. When Goliath is up, he dominates the southern sky; you can't miss him. What else would we expect of a giant?

If you read the story of David and Goliath when you looked at David's constellation, take a closer look now at the giant himself. He's heavily armed here, according to the description in I Samuel 17.

The bronze Goliath wore appears brightly everywhere; the star at the top of his head is the tip of his bronze helmet. The coat of mail gleams with bright stars at both shoulders and along his waist. The greaves (shin armor) on his legs show shiny glints at his feet.

Here Goliath has a sword in his right hand, which David later used to cut off his head. A shield is in his left hand. The Bible says the giant had a javelin slung over his back, and that's here, too. The end of the shaft passes behind his right hip and almost reaches his feet. Its gleaming bronze tip peeks over his right shoulder, which is why that point is so brilliant.

Scripture says Goliath had a shield bearer; so why is he carrying the shield himself? The young man must have been frightened by the giant's bellowing, and we can hardly blame him. If you follow the end of the javelin staff beyond his feet, you'll see the shield bearer running for dear life. Lucky for him Goliath didn't come home that night!

Goliath's pattern has been admired all over the world throughout history as the brightest in the sky. (It's a shame that honor had to go to one of the bad guys, but giants have a way of stealing the show.) It's mentioned in the Bible three times, translated "Orion" (the traditional name for it) in the same verses which speak of the Pleiades (Job 9:9; 38:31; Amos 5:8).

In these verses, the Hebrew word for this constellation means "foolishness." That means the sky's most brilliant figure is a fool—a good reminder that "God [has] made foolish the wisdom of [the] world" (I Corinthians 1:20).

In most cultures, this star group was a giant of some sort. He was usually shown as a hunter or warrior. Later Jewish tradition called him simply "the Giant," and some folks said he was Nimrod. This is probably because Nimrod was a hunter as well. Job 9:9 talks about the Giant having cords, and the story was that Nimrod was bound to the sky for rebelling against God.

The three beautiful stars in Goliath's belt have gained much attention in themselves. They've gone by many names: the Belt; the Arrow; the Line; Peter's Staff; the Yardstick; the Three Mowers; the Magi (Three Kings); and the Three Marys (Mary the mother of Jesus, Mary Magdelene, and Mary the sister of Lazarus).

The small group of stars below Goliath, which we see as his fleeing shield bearer, has been called by some Gideon's Fleece. But most often it's been know as a rabbit. The giant is hunting him, which isn't a very fair contest. Even so, he hasn't caught him yet.

Goliath lies partly in the Milky Way, and can be seen from every part of the globe. No other constellation has so many bright stars: five of second magnitude and two of first magnitude. The other first-magnitude besides Betelgeuse is *Rigel*, the blue-white star at Goliath's left foot. Like Goliath, both of these stars are giants. Rigel is thirty-three times the size of the sun and is 20,000 times more luminous. It's over 500 light-years away, so the light you see from it tonight left the star long before Columbus came to America.

Betelgeuse is even bigger in diameter, a so-called *supergiant*. It's 400 times the size of the sun, 3600 times as luminous, and about 300 light-years away.

One of the stars at the lower end of Goliath's javelin looks a little fuzzy. Binoculars would show a hazy spot around it called the *Great Orion Nebula*. A *nebula* is a vast cloud of gas and dust. Some nebulae shine with their own light, some reflect light from a nearby star, and some absorb light (so we see them as a black patch against a starry background).

This shining nebula is very thinly scattered, but it's so vast that 10,000 stars the size of our sun could be formed from the material in it. It looks tiny, however, because it's 300 light-years away.

Official names: Orion, the Hunter; Lepus, the Hare.

THE LAMB OF GOD: It's fitting that the brightest star in the sky should appear in the Lamb of God, a symbol of Jesus. If you follow the row of three stars in Goliath's armor away from his shield, you'll come across this brilliant beauty, *Sirius*. It appears on the breast of the Lamb. The other stars are much fainter, and the constellation is so far south that in our latitudes you need a clear night to see all of it.

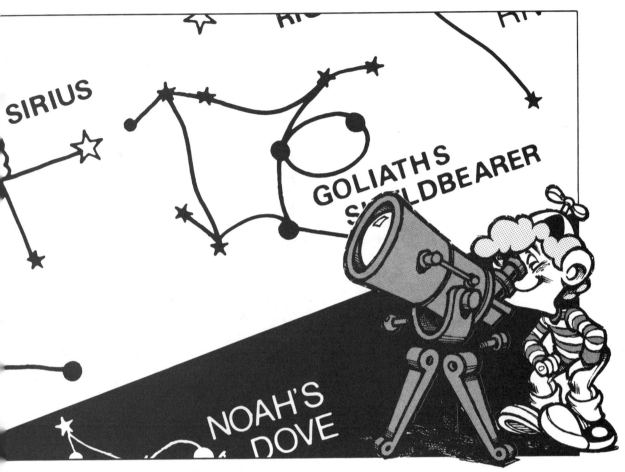

SIRIUS

GOLIATH'S SHIELDBEARER

NOAH'S DOVE

John the Baptist called Jesus the Lamb of God. That's because Christ's death on the cross was like the sacrifice of the Passover lamb. His blood made our salvation possible. You can read the story of the first Passover in Exodus 12:1-42. John's words about Jesus the Lamb of God are in John 1:29-36. Other Scriptures about Jesus as the Lamb are I Corinthians 5:7, 8; I Peter 1:18-21, and many verses in the Book of Revelation, especially chapter five.

Many ancient peoples saw this constellation as a dog. The two stars of the Flaming Sword were supposed to be his smaller companion. The dog belonged to the giant nearby and helped him hunt (making it even tougher on the rabbit). One of the early Christian astronomers, however, agreed with us that it should be the Passover lamb.

Sirius is called the Dog Star. It's one of our closest neighbors in the sky, only eight and one-half light-years away. That's what makes it the brightest star to us, even though it's only twenty-six times as luminous as the sun. This star's magnitude is so great that it's *minus 1.6*.
Official name: Canis Major, the Great Dog.

RUTH: Just off Goliath's right shoulder is a very faint group of stars in the Milky Way that wasn't made a constellation until modern times. It has no very bright members, so you may have trouble tracing it. If you can find the picture, however, imagine it as a woman standing with her arms outstretched, holding in her hand an ear of wheat. Her name is Ruth, and she is King David's great-grandmother.

Like Esther, Ruth has her own book to tell her story. Ruth didn't rescue a nation from destruction as Esther did. But she was willing to say good-bye to her own family and country and move far away in order to take care of her mother-in-law, even though they were both widows. That was a great act of courage in those days, because widows had a hard time supporting themselves. The situation was even more difficult because the people Ruth went to live with didn't like foreigners. To learn about Ruth's courage, and her happy ending, just read the book that bears her name. You'll also find out why she's holding that ear of wheat.

When this constellation was first formed, it was called the Unicorn. According to legend, unicorns were creatures of long ago that had a single horn growing from their forehead. A number of fanciful stories grew up about them during the Middle Ages. But today most people think they never existed.

The King James Version of the Bible mentions unicorns several times, but the Hebrew word there should probably be translated instead "wild beast." (See Numbers 23:22; 24:8; Job 39:9, 10; Psalm 22:21; 29:6; 92:10; and

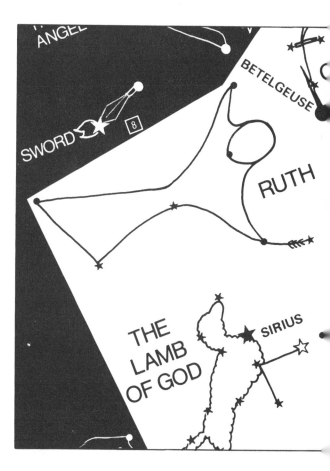

Isaiah 34:7 in the King James.) One interesting story says that unicorns died out in the Great Flood, because they refused to get on Noah's ark, but the Bible says nothing about it. Whether or not unicorns were (or still are) real, no one knows for sure. *Official name: Monoceros, the Unicorn.*

THE JORDAN RIVER: With one end near Rigel in Goliath's left foot, and the other wandering to the south, the Jordan River forms a large but faint constellation. It winds its way through a rather dull area of the sky, and its only bright member, first-magnitude *Achernar*, can be seen only in the southern states. (See chart 15.)

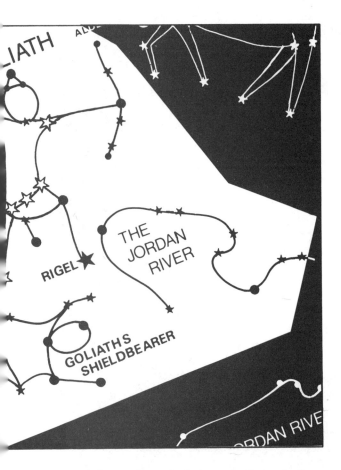

The Jordan winds its way through the Bible as well, but the area where it runs there is anything but dull. This river was the scene of great excitement when the Israelites, led by Joshua, crossed it to enter the Promised Land. On that day, a miracle took place much like the one that saved Moses and the Israelites from Pharaoh's army. To find out what happened, read Joshua chapters 3 and 4.

The Jordan was an important place in the New Testament as well. There John the Baptist came to prepare a way for Jesus' ministry. John called people to turn away from their sins and make themselves ready for the "Lamb of God," who would bring them God's forgiveness.

In many songs and poems, the Jordan River is used as a symbol of death. But it's a happy picture, because dying for the Christian is much like crossing the Jordan was for the Israelites: the long-awaited entrance into the home God has prepared for us, the "Promised Land" of Heaven.

Almost every culture has found in this long ribbon of stars the pattern of a river. Usually people called it by the name of the most important river in the region where they lived: the Nile, for example, in Egypt; the Po in Italy; and the Rhine in Germany. Early Christian astronomers called it the Jordan, as we do.

NOTE: The area of the sky around Goliath is the most beautiful in the heavens. When Goliath is high up, you can see seven stars of first magnitude in this section. Six of them form a great hexagon (six-sided figure): Capella, Pollu, Procyon, Sirius, Rigel, and Aldebaran. The seventh, Betelgeuse, is inside the figure.

On the other hand, the area outside this hexagon in the direction of Rigel is in sharp contrast, with no very bright stars. This section is called the "Wet Region," because it includes the Jordan River, Jonah's Whale, John the Baptist, and the Multiplied Fishes.

BEST TIMES to see Goliath, Ruth, and Jordan River: December through March. The Lamb of God: January through March. Whole sky charts 1-5.

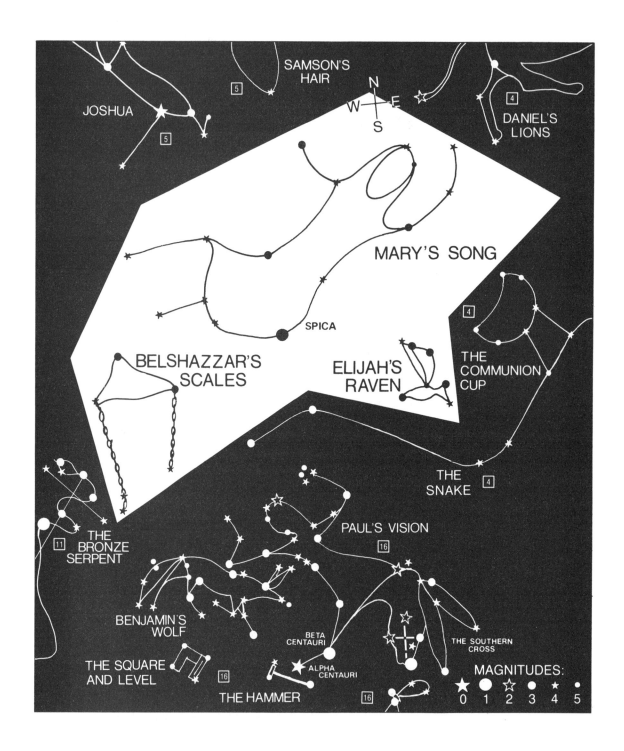

SAMSON'S HAIR

JOSHUA

DANIEL'S LIONS

MARY'S SONG

SPICA

BELSHAZZAR'S SCALES

ELIJAH'S RAVEN

THE COMMUNION CUP

THE SNAKE

THE BRONZE SERPENT

PAUL'S VISION

BENJAMIN'S WOLF

BETA CENTAURI

THE SOUTHERN CROSS

THE SQUARE AND LEVEL

ALPHA CENTAURI

THE HAMMER

MAGNITUDES:
0 1 2 3 4 5

CONSTELLATION CHART 10

MARY'S SONG: Follow the sweep of the Big Dipper's handle to Arcturus in Joshua, and then on till you reach a bright, first-magnitude star. Its name is *Spica* and it marks the left side of Mary, the mother of Jesus. The rest of her stars are fainter, but using the chart you should be able to trace out the rest of the figure. Her head is under the Lion's tail and her feet are under Joshua. She seems to be lying on her back; but if you notice that her hands are lifted over her head, you can probably guess that she's praising the Lord.

She has good reason to celebrate. In this picture, Mary just recently found out that she's to be the mother of Jesus, and she just can't contain her joy. Mary's Song is the traditional name for her beautiful words of praise on this occasion, found in Luke 1:46-55. She is also sharing the joy of her cousin, Elizabeth, who is soon to give birth to John the Baptist. To read about the unusual events surrounding this event—including a couple of visits from the angel Gabriel—read Luke 1:5-80.

Almost every culture around the world has seen in this constellation a young maiden, though she has gone by many names. Some said she was the maiden of the harvest, with a wheat spear in her hand. Others placed the nearby constellation of Scales into her hand. A few Christian astronomers saw her as Ruth gleaning the fields, and in the Middle Ages she was pictured as Mary holding the baby Jesus. One Christian astronomer, however, said this was the apostle James (the Less).

Spica is not a giant star; it's only five times the size of our sun. But it is 1000 times as luminous. Spica is about 190 light-years away. Because Mary's Song is in the Zodiac, you may see planets here, and Spica is occasionally hidden by the moon.

Spica, Arcturus (in Joshua), Cor Caroli (Nimrod's Dogs), and Denebola (Daniel's Lions) form a large diamond shape in the sky, called the *Virgin's Diamond*. (See whole sky chart 3.)

Official name: Virgo, the Virgin.

BELSHAZZAR'S SCALES: To Mary's left, just below her feet, is a rather dull star group that would be hardly known if it weren't in the zodiac. It has no bright stars, but the star lowest on its right has a very faint green color, the only green star that can be seen with the unaided eye.

This constellation has traditionally been seen as a set of scales—not the kind you stand on in the bathroom, but the kind you may have seen held by a statue with a blindfold, outside the local courthouse. (Her name is Justice.) Items were weighed out in it by placing them in a dish hanging from the chain on one side, and trying to balance them with measured weights in the dish on the other side. The dishes, however, don't appear in this star picture.

So who in the world was Belshazzar, and what was he weighing? As it turns out, Belshazzar wasn't weighing anything; he himself was being weighed—and not at the doctor's office. Evidently, he wasn't measuring up, either, because the Scales here aren't balanced.

In another exciting story from the life of Daniel, we read about how Belshazzar, who was King, gave a great banquet. But just as everyone started having a good time, something happened so scary that the Bible says the king's knees knocked together, and his legs gave way. Needless to say, the party was over. To find out what happened, and what scales have to do with all this, read Daniel 5.

Most cultures have agreed that this pattern is a set of scales, including the ancient Hebrews. Some, however, saw it only as a part of a nearby constellation. A few others have viewed it very differently: as a fire, an altar, a lamp, a censer, a dragon, a yoke, a chariot, or a crocodile. Some early Christians said it was the apostle Philip; but others agreed with us that it should be Belshazzar's Scales.

Official name: Libra, the Scales.

ELIJAH'S RAVEN: Just below Mary's head is a small but bright constellation. Two of its stars are faint, and can only be seen when the night is dark and clear. But the four brighter stars, forming a lopsided box, can easily be located. With the help of the chart, you can imagine here a raven (or crow).

We've already met the Fiery Horse who came to take Elijah to Heaven. Here we have another, much more ordinary animal God sent to serve him—a humble crow. The prophet was hiding from the king, which he often had to do, because the king didn't like what Elijah had to say. So God took care of him in a most unusual way. To discover how the raven helped this great man of God, read I Kings 17:1-6.

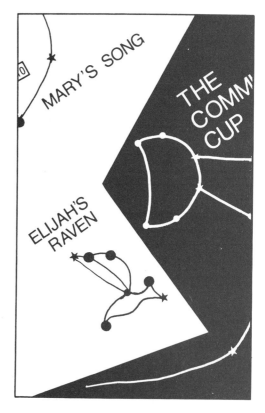

This star pattern was a raven or crow for most of the people of Europe, as well as for the Hebrews. Some said he was trying to drink out of the nearby cup. But the ancient Akkadians saw here a horse, the Arabs a camel or tent, and the Chinese a red bird. A few Christian astronomers agreed with us that it's one of Elijah's ravens, or else the one Noah sent out from the ark. But one of them combined these stars with those in the Cup to make the Ark of the Covenant.

Official name: Corvus, the Crow.

BEST TIMES to see Mary's Song and Elijah's Raven: April through June. Belshazzar's Scales: June and July. Whole sky charts 5-9.

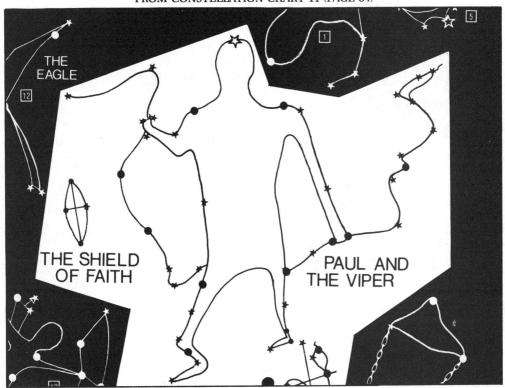

PAUL AND THE VIPER: To trace this vast and complicated figure, start with the bright star at the top of Paul's head, near the head of the King of Kings. The two pairs of stars in his shoulders are easy to recognize. Next trace the large rectangular body, and then the left arm with the Viper's front half. The Viper's head is a little grouping just south of Esther's Crown. Next trace the right arm with the Viper's tail, and finally the rather dim feet. Once you find it all, you deserve a pat on the back.

You may ask why Paul is holding a viper. In this story, the apostle was a prisoner, being shipped to Rome to stand trial. Worse yet, his ship had been wrecked in a storm, and he had just gotten to shore. So imagine his dismay when he had to wrestle with a snake as well! To find out how he met up with the viper, and who won the match, read Acts 28:1-10.

For the Greeks and Romans this constellation was the ancient doctor Asklepios. According to legend, his medicine was so powerful that he never lost a patient to death. Other peoples said he was a snake charmer from Libya. Christian astronomers of the past saw it either as we do, Paul with the viper; or as Aaron, Moses' brother whose staff became a serpent; or as Moses himself with the bronze serpent in the wilderness.

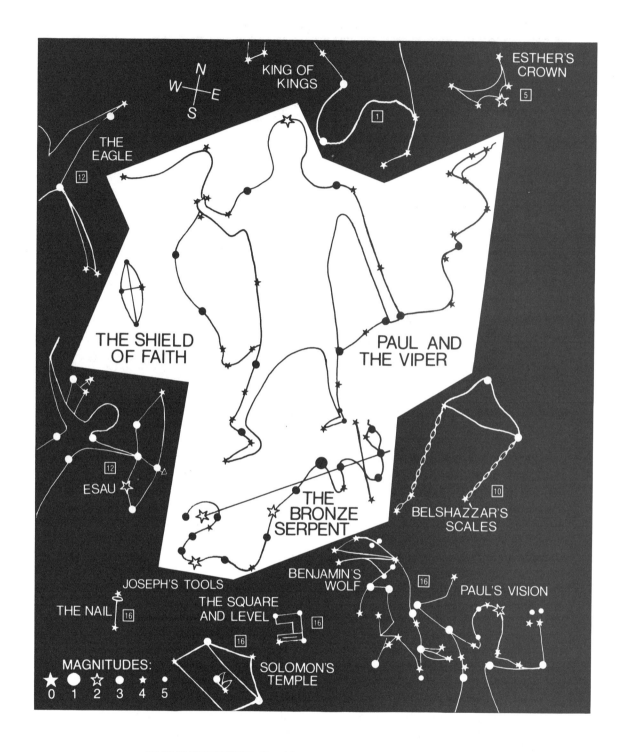

CONSTELLATION CHART 11

In the official scheme, the man and the snake are listed as separate constellations, though it is hard to look at them separately. Even more odd is the fact that this pattern reaches into the zodiac, yet tradition has never counted it as a member of that group.

Official name: Ophiuchus, the Serpent Bearer.

THE BRONZE SERPENT: This lovely constellation in the zodiac is a little too far south to be seen at its best in the northern United States. Find its brightest star, *Antares*, just below Paul's left foot. At the other end you should be able to see a close pair of stars known as the *Cat's Eyes*. Then trace the winding body, and the staff it's wrapped around, in between.

By now you must be thinking that the sky has more snakes than it needs. The reptiles certainly do make a good showing: three snakes, a lizard, and a dragon. But this beautiful snake is actually a welcome one. It doesn't bite; it heals rather than poisons; and it's another symbol of Christ.

That's certainly not an ordinary serpent, so it's well worth the time to read about how it came to be. Numbers 21:4-9 tells the story of how the Bronze Serpent was made. He was around for a long time after, till a king put an end to him in II Kings 18:1-4. But Jesus made sure he would be remembered by telling Nicodemus that this particular serpent, lifted up on the staff, was a picture of how Jesus himself would be lifted up on a cross.

That's a puzzling connection, since snakes are usually a symbol of evil. We could make many guesses about why Jesus used a serpent as a picture of himself. One reason is that everyone who looked to the bronze serpent was saved from death, just as everyone who looks to Jesus can be saved. Another clue may be Paul's words in Romans 8:3: "Sending his own Son in the likeness of sinful man to be a sin offering . . . [God] condemned sin." In any case, seeing the Bronze Serpent here in the sky can remind us of how God was faithful to save his people, both in the Old Testament and in the New.

Many traditions saw in this constellation a scorpion, and it's easy to see why. The two claws come together just above Antares, and the twisted string of stars is exactly the shape of a scorpion's body. The Hebrews saw it this way, though one Christian astronomer has claimed that in Abraham's zodiac it was an eagle.

Others have seen here a dragon, a fire, a temple, a rabbit, a sword, or a kite. Some Christians have called it the apostle Bartholomew.

Antares is first-magnitude and red. Its name means "Rival of Mars," and if that red planet wanders into this constellation, you may confuse them. Antares is another supergiant. It's 300 times the size of the sun, and more than 3000 times as luminous. If it weren't so far away—almost 300 light-years—it would shine even brighter. Like Regulus, Spica, and Aldebaran, Antares is sometimes hidden by the moon.

Official name: Scorpio, the Scorpion.

THE SHIELD OF FAITH: Beside the Viper's tail is a small and rather dull group of stars that wasn't considered a constellation until modern times. It looks like a small shield, and that has been its traditional name. We'll call it the Shield of Faith, and connect the four points to form a cross on it.

The apostle Paul tells us that we're to be wearing armor all the time. When you think of putting on armor, you may be picturing yourself like David, all weighed down with Saul's gear. But the armor Paul talks about actually makes it easier for us to move through the day. To find out what God's armor is—including the Shield of Faith—read Ephesians 6:10-18.

Official name: Scutum, the Shield.

BEST TIMES to see Paul and the Viper, the Bronze Serpent, and the Shield of Faith: July and August. Whole sky charts 7-10.

THE SHIELD OF FAITH

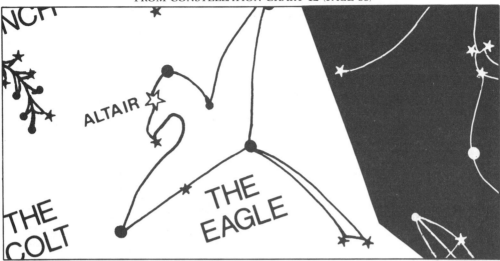

THE EAGLE: Soaring high in the heavens, with head toward the Cross and the dove of the Holy Spirit, is a majestic eagle. Its wings are outspread, and its head—formed by a row of three stars—is a landmark of the sky in summer and early fall. If you look in the right general area, you can hardly miss it.

The eagle appears throughout the Bible as a symbol of strength and swiftness. In Deuteronomy 32:11, Moses paints a beautiful picture of how the Lord took care of the Israelites the way a mother eagle cares for her young. The prophet Isaiah promises that those who hope in the Lord will renew their strength, and "soar on wings like eagles" (Isaiah 40:31). Conquering armies were also compared at times to eagles, because of their might and speed (Deuteronomy 28:49; Jeremiah 4:13; Lametations 4:19).

The eagle is probably best known in the Bible, however, as a part of two visions: one in Ezekiel and one in Revelation. In both visions, angelic creatures were seen with four faces: the face of an eagle, of an ox, of a lion, and of a man. Some people say that these four faces showed four truths about who Jesus was. The man showed that Christ was human; the ox, that he was a servant; the lion, that he was a king; and the eagle, that he was God (because the eagle soars up toward Heaven).

You can read about these visions in Ezekiel chapter 1 and Revelation chapter 4. Keep in mind as you read, though, that what these men saw is still, in many ways, a mystery. No one fully understands who these creatures are. Even so, when you see the Eagle in the night sky, you can remember that it is a symbol: of the Lord's care for his people, and of the strength he gives to those who hope in him.

Most ancient peoples, including the Hebrews, saw this constellation as an eagle or falcon. It appeared on a number of ancient coins around the Mediterranean, some with the Crab (our Angel) on the other side.

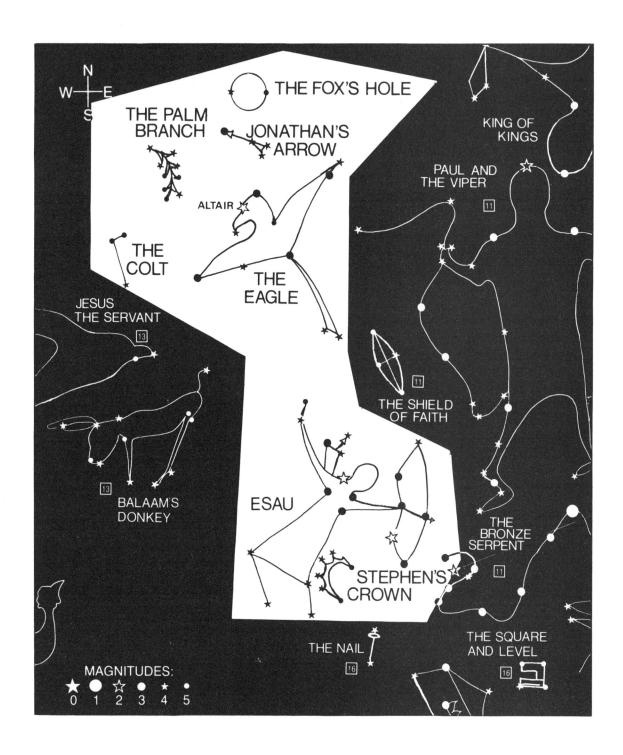

THE FOX'S HOLE

THE PALM BRANCH

JONATHAN'S ARROW

KING OF KINGS

PAUL AND THE VIPER

ALTAIR

THE COLT

THE EAGLE

JESUS THE SERVANT

THE SHIELD OF FAITH

BALAAM'S DONKEY

ESAU

STEPHEN'S CROWN

THE BRONZE SERPENT

THE NAIL

THE SQUARE AND LEVEL

MAGNITUDES:

0 1 2 3 4 5

CONSTELLATION CHART 12

The middle star in the Eagle's head is the brightest in this group. Its name is *Altair*, a yellow-white first-magnitude star. Altair is one of our closest neighbors—only sixteen light-years away. Along with Deneb (in the Cross) and Vega (in David's Lyre), it forms a huge right triangle, familiar to navigators.
Official name: Aquila, the Eagle.

ESAU: The Eagle's tail points toward a fine constellation in the southern sky: Esau, the twin brother of Jacob. The stars in his lower part are faint, and in our latitudes we often miss them because of ground haze. But the stars of the bow and body are brighter. Trace the body first by finding the four rather bright stars which form a small box, about a quarter of the size of the Big Dipper's bowl. These four are called the Milk Dipper, because they're close to the Milky Way.

Esau is carrying (not shooting) a bow and arrow in his left hand. A quiver of arrows is over his right shoulder, and his right arm is raised. Esau, the Bible says, was a skillful hunter. Right now he's out looking for some wild game to prepare for his father, Isaac.

But even though Esau will find the game he's looking for, his father won't get to eat it. Jacob and his mother have some tricks up their sleeve, and Esau is about it get cheated by his brother out of a blessing. To discover how he did it, read Genesis 27:1-41.

The ancient Hebrews called this a bow (the kind used to shoot arrows). Many other different figures have been seen here as well: an archer, a herdsman, a horseman, a centaur, an arrow, a quiver, a swan, a jester, a giant king, a horse, an elephant's tusks, a bed, ostriches, camels, a necklace, an overturned chair, a tree, and a tiger! Christian astronomers have called it Joash, King of Israel (who shot arrows out of his window); the apostle Matthew; or Ishmael, Abraham's son. The central area has been known separately as "the Teapot."

The center of our galaxy is in this direction. As you observe, watch out for planets; Esau is partly in the zodiac and partly in the Milky Way.
Official name: Sagittarius, the Archer.

JONATHAN'S ARROW: Halfway between the Cross and the Eagle, in the Milky Way, lies a small but striking constellation, Jonathan's Arrow. Though it has no bright stars, it should be easy to locate because it does look much like an arrow.

Jonathan, the son of King Saul, and David, who replaced Saul as king, were best friends. Jonathan's father was so jealous of David that he tried to kill him. Once, when David had to hide from Saul, the two friends thought of a secret way for Jonathan to send David a message. They used arrows for a special code, and this constellation shows one of those arrows. Read their story of friendship in I Samuel, chapter 20.

The ancient Hebrews also saw this little star group as an arrow, and most ancient peoples agreed it was some sort of pointed weapon. Some called it a javelin, and others a dart. Many claimed it for Cupid's arrow, which made its victim fall in love. If that's true, Paul's donkey (see chart 16) is in trouble! Christian astronomers have called it Jonathan's Arrow, as we have, while others said it was the spear or a nail used in the crucifixion of Jesus. *Official name: Sagitta, the Arrow.*

THE FOX'S HOLE: Near the foot of the Cross, next to Jonathan's Arrow, lies a very faint constellation with only two stars bright enough to show on our chart. Its official name is the Little Fox. But the pair of stars you're likely to see look more like two fox eyes, peeking out of his hole. So we'll call it the Fox's Hole, and imagine that the rest of him is hidden inside.

Once a man came to Jesus and made a bold claim. He said, "I'll follow you wherever you go." Jesus' answer to the man let him know that the Lord himself was not welcome in some places, and anyone who followed him might also be rejected.

What does the Fox's Hole have to do with this conversation? To find out, read Matthew 8:18-20. *Official name: Vulpecula, the Little Fox.*

THE PALM BRANCH: Not far from the Eagle's head is a very tiny constellation shaped like a Palm Branch. Though faint, its stars are so close together that the pattern can easily be seen on a clear, dark night.

Palm branches are an ancient symbol of honor and victory. The walls and doors of Solomon's temple in Jerusalem were decorated with palm designs (II Chronicles 3:5; I Kings 7:36). The Feast of Tabernacles, an important celebration in the ancient Jewish calendar, was held in booths made of branches from palms and other trees (Leviticus 23:39-43).

The Palm Branch has special meaning for Christians because of events that took place on the Sunday before the first Easter, when Jesus rode into Jerusalem on a donkey. To read about why this day is called Palm Sunday, see John 12:12-19.

This star group has been considered a dolphin (the mammal, not the fish) in several cultures. In ancient Arabia, however, early Christians called it the Cross of Jesus, taken up to the sky after his crucifixion. Some later Christian astronomers said it was Leviathan, the great sea creature mentioned in the Bible. Others called it Jonah's great fish, the water jars of the feast of Cana, or Job's coffin.

United States, but further north the ground haze keeps it from being visible just above the horizon.

This constellation is called Stephen's Crown for two reasons. First of all, Stephen was the first Christian martyr, which means he was the first person to die for his faith in Christ. Jesus said in Revelation 2:10: "Be faithful, even to the point of death, and I will give you the crown of life." Stephen was one of many to receive that martyr's crown of victory from the Lord.

The second reason is that Stephen's name actually means "the Crowned One." So in a very special sense, Stephen lived up to his name. To find out more about him, read Acts chapters 6 and 7. Stephen was so full of the Spirit of Christ that his death will probably remind you in many ways of Jesus' death. His final words were a powerful testimony to everyone who saw him die, and they are to us as well.

Not far from the Palm Branch, on the other side from Jonathan's Arrow, is a tiny group of stars that are barely visible. If you want to make them into a pattern, their traditional name is the Colt. It's hard to see how they resemble a young donkey (or anything else), but if you choose to see them as a colt, you can make it the colt Jesus rode on Palm Sunday.
Official names: Delphinus, the Dolphin, and Equuleus, the Colt.

STEPHEN'S CROWN: Beside Esau's feet, when he is highest in the sky, you may be able to make out a small half circle called Stephen's Crown. It can be seen rather well in the southernmost

Many cultures have called this group a crown; some Christian astronomers have also seen in it the Crown of Eternal Life, while others saw Solomon's Crown. In some lands, however, people thought it was a wheel, a bunch of arrows, a turtle, a tent, a dish, or an ostrich nest.
Official name: Corona Australis, the Southern Crown.

BEST TIMES to see the Eagle: July through October. Esau and Stephen's Crown; July and August. Jonathan's Arrow, the Fox's Hole, the Palm Branch, and the Colt: July through November. Whole sky charts 8-12.

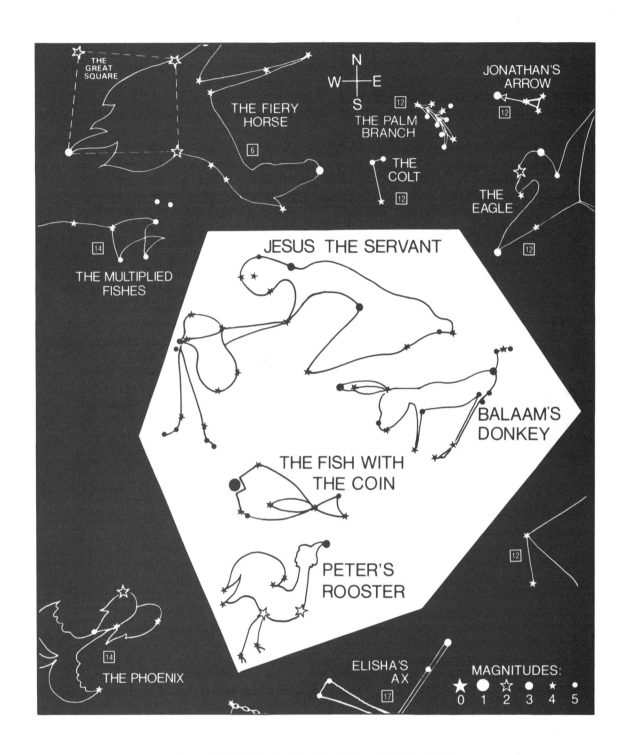

THE GREAT SQUARE

THE FIERY HORSE

6

N
W — E
S

THE PALM BRANCH

12

JONATHAN'S ARROW

12

THE COLT

12

THE EAGLE

12

THE MULTIPLIED FISHES

14

JESUS THE SERVANT

BALAAM'S DONKEY

THE FISH WITH THE COIN

PETER'S ROOSTER

12

THE PHOENIX

14

ELISHA'S AX

17

MAGNITUDES:

★ ● ☆ ● ★ •
0 1 2 3 4 5

CONSTELLATION CHART 13

BALAAM'S DONKEY: This group of stars is rather well known because it's in the zodiac. But it's so faint that if it weren't there, probably few would ever have paid much attention to it. The constellation lies in the southern sky, and is so low in northern latitudes that you'll need near-perfect conditions to make it out easily.

Look first for the three stars grouped closely together in the tail; the Eagle's head points toward them. The star on the tip of the ears lies on a straight line from Altair (in the Eagle) to Fomalhaut, a bright star in the Fish with the Coin (see below). If you think you see a very bright star in this pattern, one of the "wanderers" has fooled you.

Once you trace the outline of Balaam's Donkey, you'll find that he has his brakes on: His hooves are digging in and his head is lowered, in typical stubborn-donkey fashion. This animal had a very good reason for stopping, and his stubbornness actually saved Balaam's life. Read their story in Numbers 22:21-35, and decide for yourself which one acted more like a person that day, and which one acted like a donkey!

The Greeks and Romans called this constellation a Goatfish or a Sea Goat. Pictures show a creature with a goat's upper half, and the rest like a fish. Where it came from, and how it would be prepared in a fine restaurant, must be left to your imagination.

Other peoples saw here a normal goat, or an ibex (a kind of wild goat with long, curved horns). Christian astronomers in the past have known it as the scapegoat which Aaron the priest laid his hands on (Leviticus 16:2-22); or as Simon the Zealot, one of the twelve apostles.

Official name: Capricornus, the Sea Goat.

JESUS THE SERVANT: Draw a diagonal line across the Great Square from Peter's head to the shoulder of the Fiery Horse, and beyond. You'll run into a small group of stars which mark the head of Jesus the Servant. He is on his knees, pouring water from a jar. The stars in his body, the jar, and the water are rather faint and widely scattered, so you may need a very clear night to find them all.

Imagine how you would feel if the President of the United States came to your house to take out the garbage. That would be humbling, and you would probably insist that it wouldn't be right for him to do it. Peter felt the same way when Jesus, the Son of God who created all things, came to wash his feet. To find out what happened, read John 13:1-17.

The ancient Babylonians carved this constellation on stones as a man pouring water from a jar, and most other cultures have agreed with the picture. The Hebrews, Persians, Syrians, and Turks saw it only as the water bucket itself. Some Christians of the sixteenth and seventeenth centuries claimed it was John the Baptist, while others have seen here the apostle Jude, Naaman (the Syrian who bathed in the Jordan to be cleansed of leprosy), or Moses, drawn from the waters as a baby.

Official name: Aquarius the Water Bearer.

THE FISH W
THE CC

PETER
ROOS

14

FI

THE FISH WITH THE COIN: A line through the two bright stars on the Fiery Horse side of the Great Square, and running far down to the south, points to the brilliant star named *Fomalhaut*. When it's up, you can hardly miss it, because it's the only bright star of its kind in a very dull area. (If you find another bright star between the Great Square and Fomalhaut, it's only a planet.)

Fomalhaut is a shiny silver coin in the mouth of a fish. The faint stars which make up the fish's body are barely above the horizon in our latitudes, so you probably can't see them through the ground haze. What is a silver coin doing in a fish's mouth? The answer is in Matthew 17:24-27. Even if you don't like fishing, you may decide to go throw out a line after you read this story.

BALAAM DONKEY

Most cultures have seen this constellation as a fish. Oddly enough, many pictures show the creature drinking the water flowing out of the vessel above it (see Jesus the Servant above). Some called it the Great Fish, others the Golden Fish, still others the Southern Fish.

This star group was also the sky symbol of the ancient god Dagon of the Syrians. Dagon was pictured as having the head and hands of a man, and the body of a fish. You can read about how the Lord showed him up as a powerless idol in I Samuel 5:1-5.

Fomalhaut is blue-white and thirteen times as luminous as the sun. One of our closer neighbors, it's only twenty-two light-years away. This brilliant star announces the coming of fall. When you see it for the first time at nightfall, in mid- or late September, the leaves are beginning to turn colors. *Official name: Piscis Austrinus, the Southern Fish.*

PETER'S ROOSTER: Just south of the Fish is Peter's Rooster. In the northern part of the U.S. he only sticks his head above the horizon, and only one or two of his brighter stars can be seen. But in the southern part of the country, the whole bird can be traced when conditions are right. To learn what this noisy bird had to do with Peter, read Matthew 26:31-75.

This star pattern was not considered a constellation until modern times, when it was given the name of the Crane. This was a meaningful picture to choose, because among the ancient Egyptians the crane was the symbol for a star watcher. One Christian astronomer called it the stork mentioned by Jeremiah (8:7). The Arabs grouped it with the stars of the nearby fish. *Official name: Grus, the Crane.*

BEST TIMES to see Balaam's Donkey and Jesus the Servant: August through October. The Fish with the Coin and Peter's Rooster: September through November. Whole sky charts 9-12.

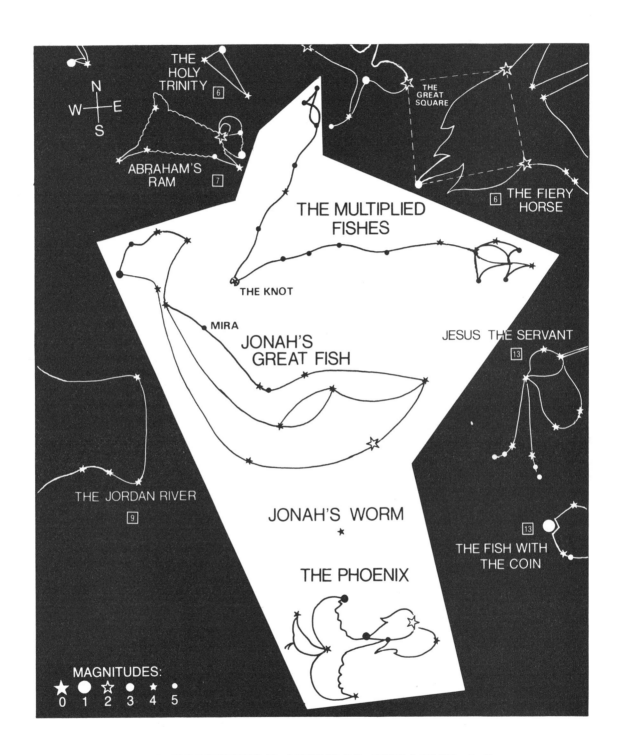

THE
HOLY
TRINITY   6

N
W   E
S

ABRAHAM'S
RAM   7

THE
GREAT
SQUARE

6   THE FIERY
HORSE

THE MULTIPLIED
FISHES

THE KNOT

MIRA

JONAH'S
GREAT FISH

JESUS THE SERVANT
13

THE JORDAN RIVER
9

JONAH'S WORM
★

THE FISH WITH
THE COIN
13

THE PHOENIX

MAGNITUDES:
★ ● ☆ ● ★ •
0 1 2 3 4 5

CONSTELLATION CHART 14

THE MULTIPLIED FISHES: The faintest constellation in the zodiac, other than the Angel, is stretched out in a great "V" shape surrounded by Abraham's Ram, Peter in Prison, the Fiery Horse, Jesus the Servant, and Jonah's Great Fish (see below). This star pattern was seen as a pair of fish by the ancient Hebrews, and by almost every other culture from earliest history. They are strung on either end of a long line, which has a knot in the middle at the point of the "V."

The Northern Fish is a small triangle of faint stars near Peter's hip. The Western Fish (also called "the Circlet") is a little brighter. It looks like a ring, just south of the Great Square. To find the Knot, draw a line from Peter's brighter foot to the Ram's head, and about the same distance beyond it.

Fish seem to swim their way into many places in the New Testament, so we could imagine these to fit several stories. But because there are two fish here, we'll use them as a picture of an unusual pair that were multiplied. Once Jesus faced a crowd of over 5,000 hungry people at dinnertime. A generous little boy offered to donate his picnic meal of five loaves of barley bread and two small fishes. The Lord took them gratefully and showed his followers that even the humble gifts of a child could be used by God in great ways. (See John 6:1-14.)

In 1524 three planets lined up close together in this constellation, which is an unusual event. A man named Stoffler announced that this would cause another great flood, like the one in Noah's day. His prediction caused many people great alarm, but that year turned out to be even drier than usual. This should be just another reminder that the heavenly bodies don't decide our future; only God does.

Official name: Pisces, the Fishes.

JONAH'S GREAT FISH: Swimming just south of the Multiplied Fishes is a very large but dim constellation, Jonah's Great Fish. His front tip is on a line from Peter's head, along the side of the Great Square, and straight on down. A second-magnitude star lies on his upper belly, and his tail points toward the Pleiades. Though the Fish's stars are faint, they still aren't hard to find, because there are few stars in this region.

No doubt you've heard the story of Jonah. But like other Bible stories, it bears reading again and again. The book that goes by his name is a very short one, only a few pages long. So when you read it, don't stop just because the prophet makes his escape. Some of the best parts of the story come later.

Did you know, for instance, that after God had appointed such a huge creature as the Fish for a special task, he also appointed one of his smallest to do a job for him? To find out who this tiny servant was, and what was its mission, read through the last chapter of Jonah. If you want to place it in the sky, too, you can say it's in the group of faint stars wiggling below the Great Fish's belly. (All but one of the members of this group are too faint to show up on our chart.)

The constellation we see as Jonah's Great Fish has also been known as a

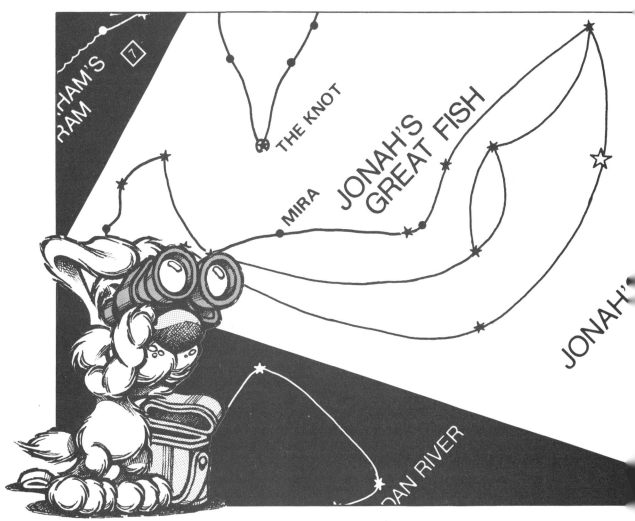

THE KNOT

MIRA

JONAH'S GREAT FISH

JONAH'

DAN RIVER

whale and as a sea monster. In that picture, the monster is coming to eat the princess being sacrificed to him in the nearby constellation called Andromeda, which we call Peter in Prison. When this star pattern is pictured as a monster, what we see as the tail is often viewed instead as an ugly head on a long neck.

Christian astronomers of the past have said this was either Jonah's fish, or the sea monster named Leviathan. Some modern star watchers have called it

the Easy Chair, with its back leaning toward Gideon's Bull. But only a very trusting soul would turn his back toward an animal with horns like that.

The Great Fish has a famous variable star called *Mira*. In 331 days it changes from tenth-magnitude (invisible without a telescope) to third-magnitude and back. Most of the time you can't see it. The faint star at the tip of the Fish's flipper is *Tau Ceti*, the third-nearest star which can be seen in our latitudes with the unaided eye.

98

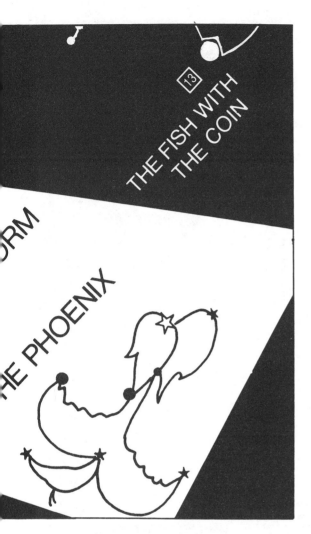

THE FISH WITH THE COIN

THE PHOENIX

The Phoenix is an imaginary creature and is not mentioned in the Bible, but we've kept the traditional name for an important reason. The legend of the Phoenix says that it was a large, beautiful bird which built a nest every 500 years. Then it would set the nest on fire and burn itself alive. From the flames, however, the Phoenix would always rise again in new life. So from ancient times this bird, though not a real one, has been a symbol of resurrection and of everlasting life.

Though none of the biblical authors wrote about the Phoenix legend, Clement, one of the apostle Peter's disciples, did. Clement was a great leader of the early church, and the head of the church at Rome. His letters were read and passed around from one church to another, like the letters of Paul. In fact, early Christians respected his writings almost as much as the Scriptures themselves.

In one of his letters to the Corinthians, written about 95 or 96 A.D., Clement uses the story of the Phoenix to teach about the resurrection and eternal life of believers in Jesus. Ever since then, this bird has been used by Christians as a symbol of our life with the Lord after we die.

For that reason, the Phoenix is a worthy figure to include. Even though the legend itself is not described in Scripture, the hope it illustrates is at the very heart of the Bible.

Official name: Phoenix, the Phoenix.

Only Sirius and Procyon are closer. Tau Ceti is about ten light-years away.

Official names: Cetus, the Sea Monster; Sculptor, the Sculptor.

THE PHOENIX: South of the Great Fish is a constellation known as the Phoenix. Like Peter's Rooster, it only appears in part above the horizon as seen from the northern U.S. But in the far south of the country, it can be seen whole when conditions are right.

BEST TIMES to see Jonah's Great Fish and the Multiplied Fishes: October through January. The Phoenix: Nov.-Jan. Whole sky charts 1, 9-12.

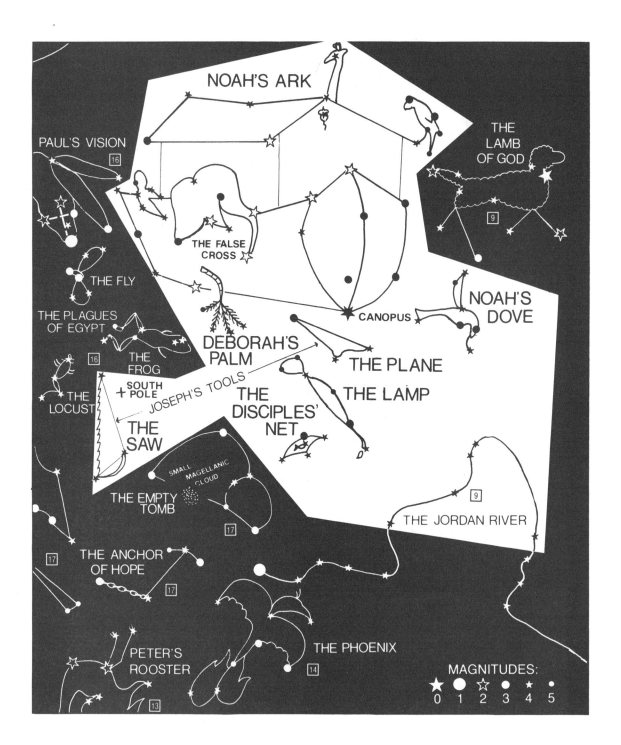

NOAH'S ARK

THE LAMB OF GOD

9

PAUL'S VISION

16

THE FLY

THE PLAGUES OF EGYPT

16

THE FROG

THE LOCUST

THE FALSE CROSS

CANOPUS

NOAH'S DOVE

DEBORAH'S PALM

SOUTH POLE

JOSEPH'S TOOLS

THE SAW

THE DISCIPLES' NET

THE PLANE

THE LAMP

SMALL MAGELLANIC CLOUD

THE EMPTY TOMB

17

9

THE JORDAN RIVER

THE ANCHOR OF HOPE

17

17

PETER'S ROOSTER

13

THE PHOENIX

14

MAGNITUDES:

0 1 2 3 4 5

CONSTELLATION CHART 15
The Southernmost Constellations, I

The constellations shown on charts 15 through 17 lie near the south pole of the sky. In middle latitudes—including much of the United States—most of these groups are out of sight altogether. The further south you go, however, the more of them you can see. If you pass the equator, you can see all of them at one time or another. So if you're planning a trip south, be sure to take this book along.

Except for Noah's Ark, Paul's Vision, Benjamin's Wolf, and Solomon's Temple, these groups were not even seen as constellations until modern times. Many of the stars are faint, few, and far between—so you'll have to use your imagination a little more when picturing these. The chart illustrations cheat a little—they add in a few lines where the sky has no stars. But overall, you should be able to see patterns that look at least a little like their names, and you can probably think of some that fit even better.

NOAH'S ARK is a large and majestic group of stars. It's not too hard to trace when it floats high enough in the sky. The bow of the ship is just behind the Lamb of God, headed in the same direction. Its most famous star, *Canopus*, is at the bottom of the bow, where it touches the water.

There are so many stars here that you can have a great time matching them up with animals of every sort. The chart shows the small group at the stern as Noah, his hand stretched over the side. The dove is flying beyond the bow, with an olive branch in its mouth. You can add an elephant, giraffe, parrot, and mice, as shown here (lots of imagination needed); or make up

your own zoo collection. You can read the story in Genesis 6—9.

The Ark or Ship is also an ancient symbol of the Church. A letter that is said to be written by Clement says: "The whole business of the Church is like a great ship, carrying through a violent storm people from many places, who want to live in the city of the good kingdom [of heaven]."

This star group is officially made up of four constellations, though the ancients pictured them as we do, all together as one. To make it easier for astronomers to label the stars, they have been divided into the Sail, the Keel, the Stern, and the ship's Compass. The dove, which we include in the group as well, is also officially its own constellation. The modern astronomer who formed this little group actually named it in honor of Noah's dove.

The Greeks said this was the Argo, the ship which took Jason on his quest for the Golden Fleece in the ancient legend. Most other peoples have agreed that it's a ship, some saying it was the first to sail the ocean. Others have called it a pirate ship. One African tribe saw things a little differently, however; they insisted it was a horse.

Canopus is second only to Sirius in brightness. It's yellow-white, is 2000 times as luminous as the sun, and lies 100 light-years away. You can see this beauty from the most southern states, and may even get a glimpse of it as far north as Tennessee.

The group of four stars which we show connected by dotted lines in the

101

elephant's head have been called the False Cross because they're often mistaken for the Southern Cross, a nearby constellation which we've made part of Paul's Vision (see chart 16).

Official names: Argo Navis, the Ship Argo, made up of Carina, the Keel; Puppis, the Stern; Vela, the Sail; and Pyxis, the Compass. Also Columba, the Dove.

DEBORAH'S PALM: Crossing over into the hull of the Ark is a small, faint star group. If you try hard, you can think of it as an upside-down palm tree.

The U.S. Supreme Court has had its first woman justice appointed, and female judges are becoming more and more common in other American courts as well. But in ancient Israel, a woman judge was highly unusual. In fact, we're only told about one in the Old Testament, and her name was Deborah.

Deborah used to hold court under a tree called Deborah's Palm. Actually, she *was* the court; and she was a leader of the people in other ways as well. To read about Deborah, turn to Judges chapter 4.

Like most of the extreme southern constellations, this one is a modern creation. It is commonly known as the Flying Fish, which explorers from Europe saw in tropical waters as they sailed to the New World. But some have called it a sparrow, and one Christian astronomer grouped it with the Dolphin (our Lamp) to make Abel, Adam and Eve's son.

Official name: Volans, the Flying Fish.

JOSEPH'S TOOLS: Scattered around the southern end of the sky are several small and simple constellations which we have called Joseph's Tools. Two of them appear on this chart: the Saw (right next to the South Pole, which is marked on the chart with a small "x"), and the Plane (just below the bow of the Ark). Both of these patterns are only simple triangles, but they do look a little like their namesakes. To find the other tools (the Hammer, the Nail, and the Carpenter's Square and Level combined), see chart 16.

We don't know much about Joseph, Mary's husband, who helped her raise Jesus as a boy. We know that he was a carpenter by trade, and that's why his tools appear here. But we can only guess that Joseph had died by the time

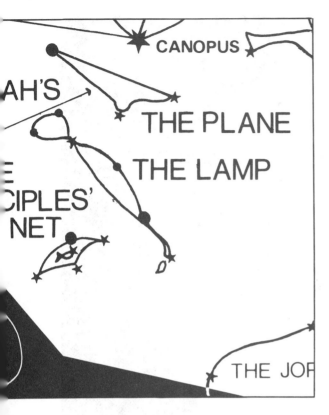

CANOPUS

AH'S

THE PLANE

THE LAMP

CIPLES'
NET

THE JO

THE LAMP: Just below Joseph's plane is a group of stars a little narrower and longer. Its shape is roughly like an ancient oil lamp, with the handle pointing toward Deborah's Palm.

The Lamp has long been a symbol of wisdom, because it gives off light to show people their way in the darkness. For that reason, too, the Word of God is called in the Psalms "a lamp to my feet and light for my path" (Psalm 119:105).

Jesus told a story once about ten young women at a wedding, each one with a lamp. Five of them were wise, five were foolish; and the difference between them was how they took care of their lamps. To find out what happened to each group, read Matthew 25:1-13.

This constellation was named in modern times as a dolphin (the fish, not the mammal). Others called it a swordfish.

Official name: Dorado, the Dolphin.

Jesus began his ministry—the last time he's mentioned in the Bible, Jesus was only twelve years old.

This scattered group of faint constellations were given names in modern times: the Saw, as we call it, was called an octant (a device to help in navigation); the Plane, a painter's easel; the Hammer, a compass; the Nail, a telescope; and the Square and Level constellation has kept its original name. None of them have very bright stars. The South Pole of the sky, which is not marked by a star the way the North Pole is marked by Polaris, lies closest to the Saw.

Official names: Pictor, the Easel, and Octans, the Octant.

THE DISCIPLES' NET: Near the upper rim of the Lamp is a tiny diamond pattern of stars, known traditionally as the Net. We'll call it the Disciples' Net, because we often find these men fishing in stories from the New Testament. (The lone star inside the diamond can be a little fish.)

Read two great fish stories (true ones) in Luke 5:1-11 and John 21:1-14.

Official name: Reticulum, the Net.

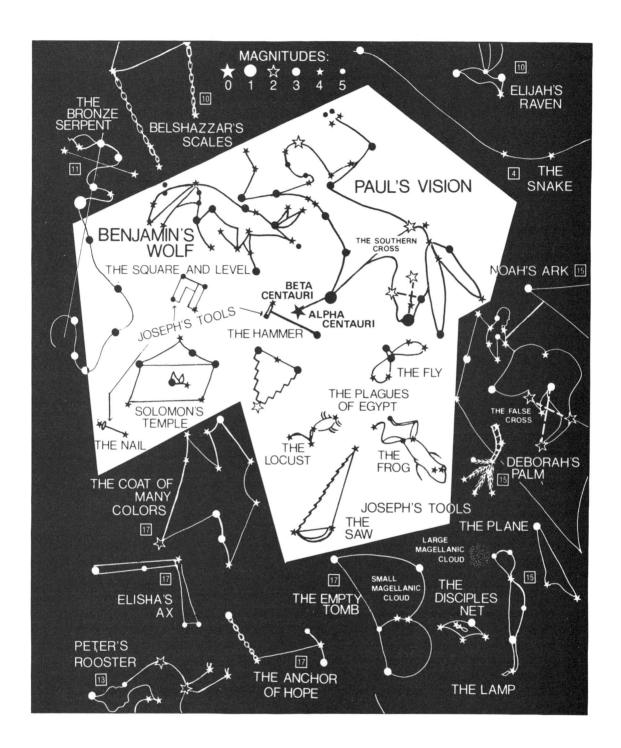

MAGNITUDES:
0 1 2 3 4 5

THE BRONZE SERPENT

BELSHAZZAR'S SCALES

ELIJAH'S RAVEN

THE SNAKE

PAUL'S VISION

BENJAMIN'S WOLF

THE SQUARE AND LEVEL

THE SOUTHERN CROSS

NOAH'S ARK

JOSEPH'S TOOLS

BETA CENTAURI

ALPHA CENTAURI

THE HAMMER

THE FLY

THE FALSE CROSS

DEBORAH'S PALM

SOLOMON'S TEMPLE

THE NAIL

THE PLAGUES OF EGYPT

THE LOCUST

THE FROG

JOSEPH'S TOOLS

THE PLANE

THE COAT OF MANY COLORS

THE SAW

LARGE MAGELLANIC CLOUD

ELISHA'S AX

THE EMPTY TOMB

SMALL MAGELLANIC CLOUD

THE DISCIPLES NET

THE LAMP

PETER'S ROOSTER

THE ANCHOR OF HOPE

CONSTELLATION CHART 16
The Southernmost Constellations, II

PAUL'S VISION: A large, striking figure, though a bit complicated to trace, lies just below the southern end of the Snake. It was known to the Greeks as a half-man, half-horse creature (a centaur), but we'll see it instead as a man falling off his donkey. Locate first the four bright stars in the donkey's head (the Southern Cross, as they're called); the one in the rider's head; and the two in his bended leg. Then fill in the rest of the figure from there.

Saul (another name for the apostle Paul) was a violent and angry man. He thought that Christians were overturning Jewish faith and traditions; so he went around looking for them, to throw them into prison. While Paul was on his way to round up some more Christians in the city of Damascus, so he could bring them back as prisoners to Jerusalem, God changed Paul's heart. Read about this unusual event in Acts 9:1-19.

Though the Greeks saw a centaur here, others called it a full horse, a bull, or a *minotaur* (half man, half bull). In the Middle Ages it was often called Noah; later a Christian astronomer said it was Abraham with Isaac.

Alpha Centauri is the star at Paul's foot. It's first-magnitude and yellow, the brightest of all near stars (only 4.3 light-years away). Alpha Centauri is actually a double star, two stars moving around each other. The larger of the two is only a little bigger and brighter than our sun.

The star at Paul's knee is *Beta Centauri*, blue and not quite as bright as its companion. It's 190 light-years away, and 1500 times as luminous as the sun.

But Alpha looks brighter to us because it's so much closer.

The *Southern Cross*, in the donkey's head, was long ago part of the larger constellation, as we have it. But now it's officially its own constellation. Even so, because we already have a Cross in the north, and a donkey needs a head, we've used these stars to help Paul out. Some say it looks more like a kite than a cross anyway, and it's not nearly as beautiful as the Cross in the northern sky. It can be seen about as far north as Key West, Florida.

The Southern Cross has two first-magnitude stars, both blue. One is *Acrux* (or Alpha Crucis), a double star, 270 light-years away. The pair combined is about 1400 times as luminous as the sun. *Becrux* (or Beta Crucis) is 500 light-years away, sending out 850 times as much light as the sun.

Just to the east of the bottom of the cross is a large dark area, a region of dust. It's called the Coal Sack.

Official names: Centaurus, the Centaur; Crux, the Southern Cross.

JOSEPH'S TOOLS: For a description of the full set, see chart 15. The Hammer, Nail, and Square and Level appear scattered across this chart. The Saw and the Plane are both here and in chart 15.

Official names: Circinus, the Compass; Telescopium. the Telescope; Norma [et Regula], the Square [and Level].

THE TOWER OF BABEL: Below Alpha Centauri in Paul's Vision is a triangle shape, larger and brighter than the triangle in the northern sky (the Holy Trinity). Imagine that this triangle has terraced sides, with steps going up to the top. You'll be picturing an ancient *ziggurat*, the kind of building many historians think the Tower of Babel was intended to be.

Have you ever wondered why everyone on earth doesn't speak the same language? Actually, the Bible says there *was* a time when all people spoke the same language. To find out why they don't anymore, read the story of the Tower of Babel in Genesis 11:1-9.

This constellation is known as the Southern Triangle. One early Christian astronomer called it the Three Patriarchs—Abraham, Isaac, and Jacob.

Official name: Triangulum Australe, the Southern Triangle.

THE PLAGUES OF EGYPT: Leaping, buzzing, and hopping around the sky among the other southernmost constellations are an odd combination of little creatures: a frog, a fly, and a locust. You may need a little extra help to imagine these stars in their shapes, so we've added a few extra lines in the chart diagrams.

Frogs are usually harmless little guests to have around the yard. But imagine how it would be to have them swarm in by the thousands—in your bed, your oven, your drinking glasses, even your hair. Worse yet, think how it would be if they all died without leaving first.

That's exactly what happened to the ancient Egyptians. When Pharaoh—whose Chariot is in the northern sky—

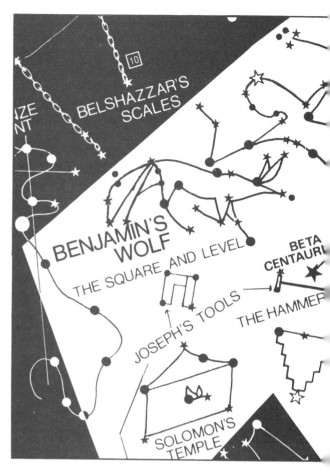

refused to let the Hebrews leave the country, the Lord sent an army of frogs to pester them. In fact, God had to send troubles, or *plagues*, on the whole Egyptian nation *ten times* before Pharaoh would agree to let Moses lead the people out. One of the other times, God sent swarms of flies; another time, he sent locusts. That's why these three creatures are here together, called the Plagues of Egypt. (Another plague was darkness, so if you like, you can choose any black patch of sky nearby and add it to this constellation.) To find out what six other plagues the Egyptians had to suffer before Pharaoh would give in, read Exodus 7:14—12:32.

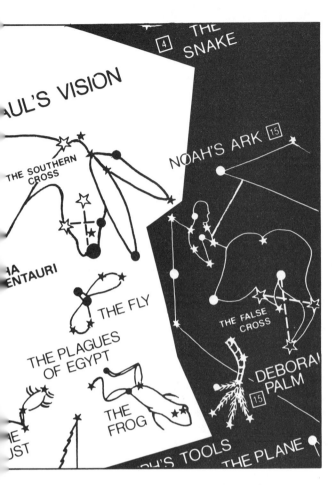

one is the symbol of Jacob's son Benjamin, the father of one of the twelve tribes of Israel. To learn why this is Benjamin's symbol, read Genesis chapter 49, where Jacob is predicting what each of his sons and their tribes will be like.

Wolves are known for their boldness, fierceness, and greediness in eating. They'll often kill much more than they can eat or take away, and they're an enemy especially of sheep. Since the people of God are sometimes called his sheep, the wolf has long been a symbol of those who would destroy the Church.

But one Scripture about the Wolf can give us hope. The prophet Isaiah wrote about the new age to come, when Jesus will reign and his people will enjoy peace. Isaiah described that time in poetry by saying that "the wolf will live with the lamb" (Isaiah 11:6). His picture encourages us that even those who have long been enemies will at last live together without fear of one another. If for no other reason, then, we should be glad to have a Wolf in the sky. He's a sign to us that someday we'll live together in God's kingdom of peace.

The Greeks and Romans called this constellation simply the Beast, without further description. Some Arabs insisted that it was a lioness or leopard, while others claimed it was a monster. One ancient writer called it a wineskin, though the flask must have had either an odd shape or lots of bright holes. Somewhere along the way, however, someone named it the Wolf, and the title stuck.

Official name: Lupus, the Wolf.

Traditional names for these three constellations are the Chameleon, the Fly, and the Bird of Paradise (a flower that looks something like a bird of the same name).

Official names: Chameleon, the Chameleon; Musca, the Fly; Apus, the Bird of Paradise.

BENJAMIN'S WOLF: Trotting along beneath Paul's right elbow is a group of stars that look much like a wolf. Though wolves aren't usually welcome—on earth or in the sky—this

SOLOMON'S TEMPLE: In between the Bronze Serpent and the Tower of Babel are six stars that look a little like a leaning house. Inside are two more stars, which many ancient peoples imagined as a fire.

We will call it the Temple of King Solomon. And it's probably leaning because it was built on a hill, Mount Moriah in Jerusalem. The two stars inside are the flame of the cedar altar in the inner court of the temple, which Solomon overlaid with gold. When seen from our half of the globe the whole structure is standing on its roof. You can find details of how the temple was built in II Chronicles 3, 4, and you can read more about Solomon in II Chronicles 1 and I Kings 10, 11.

This constellation has been known as an altar, a hearth, a brazier, or a censer (a vessel for burning incense). All of these pictures viewed the two stars in the middle as a flame.

Official name: Ara, the Altar.

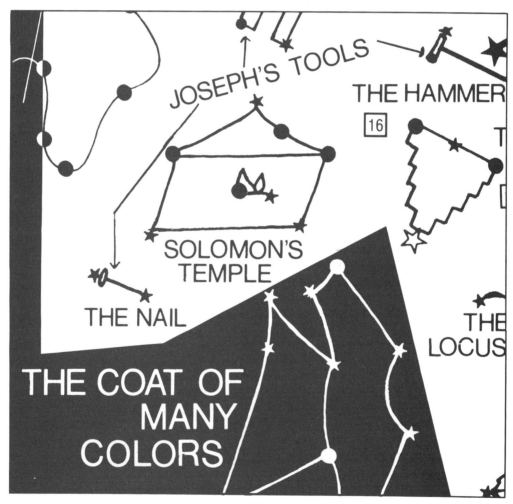

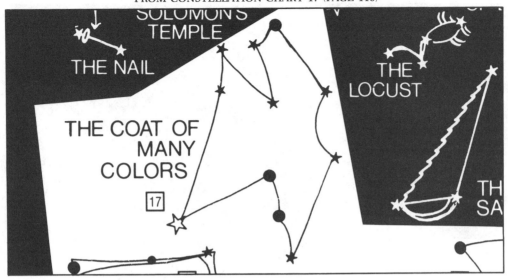

THE COAT OF MANY COLORS: On the side of the Tower of Babel opposite Paul is a group of stars that forms a jacket of sorts. With the help of the chart, imagine the two full sleeves and a broad neck, with a long, flowing body. Stretch your imagination a little more by adding a rainbow of colors to the coat's fabric. You now have the Coat of Many Colors, Jacob's gift to his favorite son, Joseph.

This coat made Joseph's brothers terribly jealous of him. Most brothers and sisters feel a little jealousy toward each other, at one time or another. Sometimes they believe that Mom or Dad likes one child better than the other. But Joseph's brothers were more than a little jealous; they felt so strongly that they were ready to kill him. To find out how Joseph escaped from their plot—and had an amazing adventure in a faraway place instead—read Genesis chapter 37.

Joseph's full story in Genesis 37—50 is really a series of stories, each with its own interesting plot and useful lessons. (Chapter 38, however, is about someone else.) This young man's life was one surprise after another, all of them leading up to a special plan God had in mind for taking care of his family.

This constellation was named in modern times the Peacock. If you want to imagine it that way, it still is an important symbol: From ancient times this bird, like the Phoenix, has been a sign of resurrection and everlasting life. No one is sure why the peacock has that symbolic meaning. But it may be because many years ago, people thought the flesh of the peacock did not decay, but rather stayed always fresh and sweet. Another reason may be that when the peacock molts, the feathers he grows back are said to be more brilliant than the ones he lost. In the same way, our new life in heaven will be much better than our life on earth.

Official name: Pavo, the Peacock.

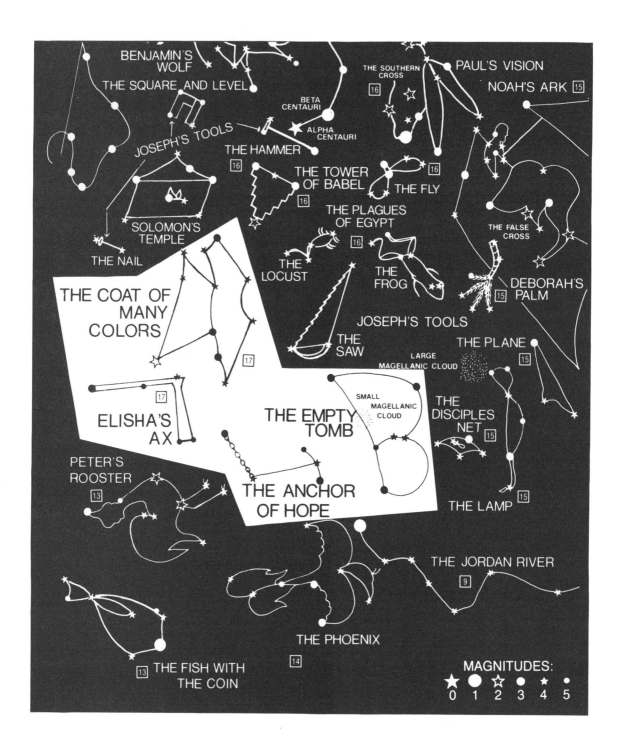

CONSTELLATION CHART 17
The Southernmost Constellations, III

THE EMPTY TOMB: Not far from the Net, on the side opposite the Lamp, is a somewhat larger star group. If you imagine the stars on one end as an arched doorway, and the stars on the other end as a round stone, you'll see the Empty Tomb. The stone has been rolled away from the door.

This Tomb reminds us of the most joyful day in all history: the morning when Jesus rose from the dead. The story of that first Easter never grows old, because it is our proof that Jesus is Lord—even over death. To read again about that exciting event, turn to Matthew chapter 28.

This constellation was named in modern times the Water Snake. One Christian astronomer combined its stars with those in the Anchor of Hope (chart 16) to make the angel Raphael. (Raphael, the angel of healing, isn't mentioned in our Bible, but he appears in some very old and respected Jewish books called the *Apocrypha*.)

Official name: Hydrus, the Water Snake.

Achernar is a brilliant blue first-magnitude star at the southern end of the Jordan River, near the Empty Tomb (see chart 9 for a description of the River). It's seventy light-years away, and is 200 times as luminous as the sun, At the right times it can be seen from the states furthest south.

A special sight in this area are the two *Magellanic Clouds*, the Larger and the Smaller. The Larger lies between the Lamp and the Empty Tomb; the Smaller is at the bottom of the Tomb's door. These faint silvery patches are galaxies made of millions of stars, and move around our own galaxy, the Milky Way. To see them well, you have to cross the equator.

ELISHA'S AX: Beyond the left sleeve of the Coat of Many Colors is a simple constellation that looks like a triangle attached to a stick. It's an ax, but it's not just any ax.

Elisha was the man Elijah prepared to follow in his footsteps. Like his teacher, this prophet healed the sick, raised the dead, and multiplied food. But he also made an iron axhead float. To discover how, read II Kings 6:1-7.

This constellation is commonly known as the Indian (Native American). At most it looks like a tomahawk.

Official name: Indus, the Indian.

THE ANCHOR OF HOPE: Our last constellation appears near the Empty Tomb, the Phoenix, and the Jordan River. The River is a symbol of death; the Tomb, of Jesus' resurrection; and the Phoenix, of our resurrection. So there could be no more fitting place to find the Anchor of Hope, for the great hope of the Christian is eternal life with the Lord.

This figure comes from Hebrews 6:19. There the writer tells us that hope is our anchor. Our lives may be tossed about by troubles, but we can remain firm in our faith that at the end of our journey, God will bring us safely home.

Officially, this constellation is a toucan, the odd-looking fowl which the Chinese fittingly call the "Beak Bird."

Official name: Tucana, the Toucan.

MAKE YOUR OWN PICTURE: THE MILKY WAY

Stretched through the sky across many constellations is a band of light commonly known as the Milky Way. The Milky Way is not a constellation; it's actually made of the combined light of millions of stars which are too faint to be seen individually with the unaided eye. But any book about the stars would be incomplete without at least a few words about it, so be sure to look for it. You'll need a dark and clear night; moonlight or haze can easily blot the Milky Way out from sight.

Our sun belongs to a vast system of stars called a *galaxy*, which is shaped like a disk and turning around its center. We call it the Milky Way Galaxy. When we see the Milky Way stretched across the sky, we are actually looking out at our own galaxy sideways. Because of our viewpoint, it looks more like a narrow strip than a round disk. Try looking at a dinner plate from the edge instead of the top to get a general idea of the angle.

Such a beautiful sight could, of course, not escape notice by people everywhere, all through history. So the Milky Way has had many names around the world, and has been talked about in countless legends, stories, and poems. The ancient Hebrews called it the River of Light. Others have called it the River of Heaven, the Silver River, the Great Serpent, the Path of the Snake, the Heavenly Belt, the Castle, the Tracks of the Sun, the Path of Noah's Ark, the Dove of Paradise, the Circle of Milk, the Court of God, the Path of Ashes, the Path of Straw, the Birds' Way, the Winter Street, the Pilgrim's Road, Jacob's Road, Jacob's Ladder, and the Road to Heaven.

With so many pictures to choose from, we'll leave to you the task of deciding which one suits the Milky Way best. Or better yet, think of your own. If you want to match it up with a Bible story or character, just get a good concordance and look up a key word from your picture, such as "road" or "belt." Then you can choose which one it will show. For example, The Road to Emmaus (Luke 24:13-35) or Jeremiah's Belt (Jeremiah 13:1-11) would work well for this one.

If you've enjoyed learning about these pictures, you'll probably enjoy creating others of your own as well. A journal or notebook with blank pages will help. You can draw dots for the stars as you see them, using a pen. Then try different ways of connecting them to make a figure, using a pencil so you can erase. Remember: There are no right or wrong pictures, so enjoy yourself. The sky's the limit!

III
PUTTING IT ALL TOGETHER

HOW TO USE THE WHOLE SKY CHARTS

Once you've learned the shapes of individual constellations, it's time to put them all together into maps of the whole sky. These charts are the ones you should use when you go outside to observe. The whole sky charts are double. The left-hand charts show the stars the way they appear in the heavens; the right-hand charts show the same stars, connected with lines to show the constellations.

At the bottom of each chart are a date and hour. The chart shows how the sky would look at that date and hour from a latitude of 40° north. The parts of the sky farthest north and south which you see from your location will differ more or less from this chart, according to how far away you live from that latitude. But most of the sky is the same throughout the latitudes of the United States.

To make adjustments for different dates or hours, follow these guidelines:

We give a chart for the first day of each month, which can be used for the two weeks surrounding that date. For example, the chart for January 1 can be used for the last week of December and the first week of January.

If, however, you are observing in the *middle* of the month (from around the 8th to the 23rd), you can adjust by using the same chart, but keeping in mind that the stars will be in this position somewhat *earlier* in the evening (an hour earlier on the 15th). Chart 1, for example, can still be used for mid-January, but it shows how the stars will appear from 6-8 p.m., rather than 7-9 p.m.

These charts are given for 7-9 p.m., which are the most likely hours for families to be star watching. If you are out *later* than these hours, simply use the *following* chart. For example, if it's January 1 and you're using Chart 1, after 9 p.m. you would use Chart 2 instead. (If it is December 1 and you're using Chart 12, after 9 p.m. go to Chart 1.) And if you stay out even later—past 11 p.m.—simply go on to the next chart, and so on through the night, changing charts every two hours.

Of course, in the winter months you may be out *earlier* than 7 p.m. If so, simply go to the chart immediately *before* the one for that date. For example, if you are out at 6 p.m. on February 1, use Chart 1 instead of Chart 2. (If it is January 1, use Chart 12 instead of Chart 1.)

To make an adjustment for *both* date and hour, begin by finding the chart for the first day of the right month. If you are now in the middle of the month, the chart will show how the sky looks from about 6-8 p.m. So if you're out earlier than 6 p.m., go to the *preceding* chart. If you're out later, go to the *following* chart. Then move forward one chart every two hours throughout the evening. If it is the last week of the month, however, use the chart for the first day of the next month, and make adjustments for time as already described.

118

Some stars and constellations extend beyond the circle (inscribing the area of sky visible from 40° north latitude). These are for the benefit of people farther north or south.

To warn you of the areas where planets might be wandering, we've added a white dotted line to the whole sky charts along the ecliptic. The planets will never stray very far from that path. So if you see an extra, brilliant star near this path, you've probably found a planet. They're beautiful to observe, too.

Before you go outside, take a look at the constellations in the right-hand charts, and then try to find them in the left-hand charts. Use this as a practice exercise. It will make things much easier when you look at the real sky.

When you take these charts outside to watch, find north first by locating the Polestar from the Big Dipper. The stars in the north are the same all through the year, so you'll be familiar with them soon. As you look north, turn the book so that the word "north" on the chart reads right side up (likewise for looking in the other directions).

Begin looking in the west, because the western stars are setting. If you wait until you've looked at the rest of the sky, some of them will be gone. Look for the brightest stars first; then for the brightest constellations; and then for the fainter ones. If you want more details about a constellation you're looking at, the number near its name tells you where it's found in the biblical constellation charts.

Have you ever noticed that the sun and moon look much larger near the horizon than they do higher up? The same is true of the constellations; they seem to shrink as they rise. Keep that in mind as you watch.

One final note: As we see them from earth, all stars have the same size—they're only pinpoints of light. But they do differ in brightness. On the biblical constellation charts, this difference is shown by a series of six symbols. **On the whole sky charts, we have indicated just two different symbols: ☆ for first- and second-magnitude stars and • for all stars of lesser magnitude. But remember that the stars won't look as big or as close together as these symbols would suggest.**

WHOLE SKY CHART 1

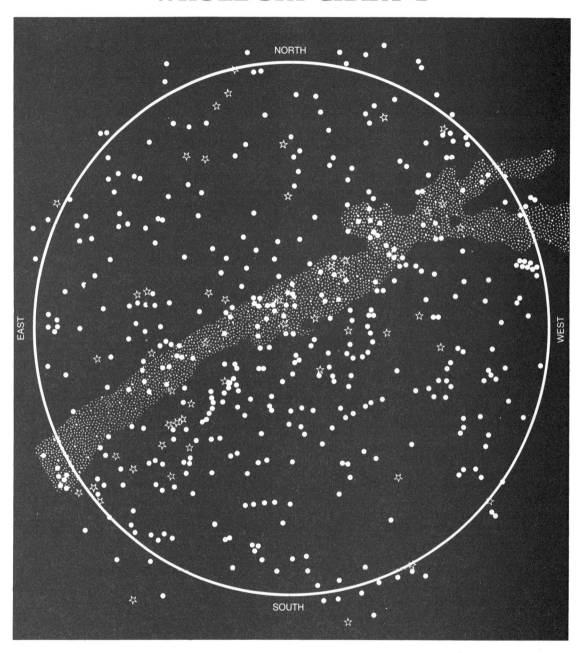

☆ Stars of first- or
 second-magnitudes (or brighter)
● All stars of lesser magnitude

Numbers in chart at right refer
to Constellation Charts 1-17.

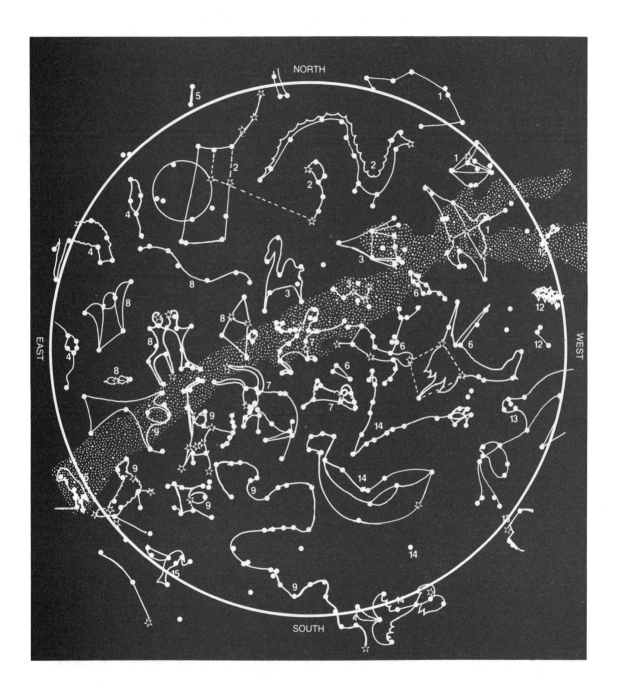

January 1: 7-9 p.m.

To adjust for differing date or hour, see instructions on page 118.

121

WHOLE SKY CHART 2

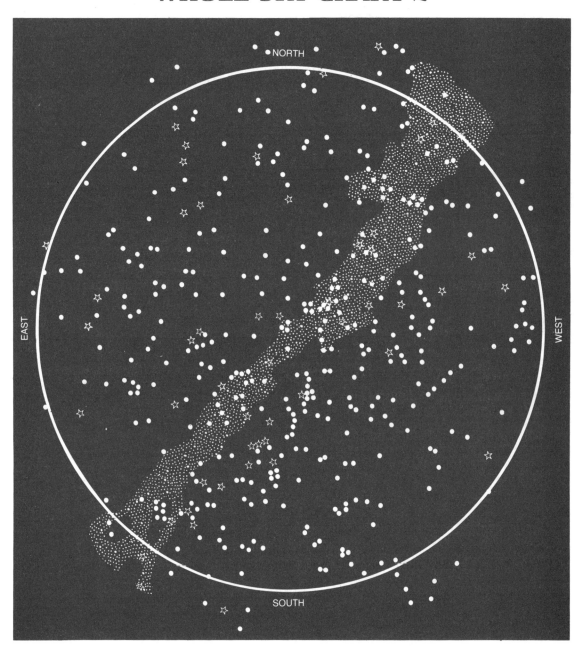

☆ Stars of first- or
second-magnitudes (or brighter)

● All stars of lesser magnitude

Numbers in chart at right refer
to Constellation Charts 1-17.

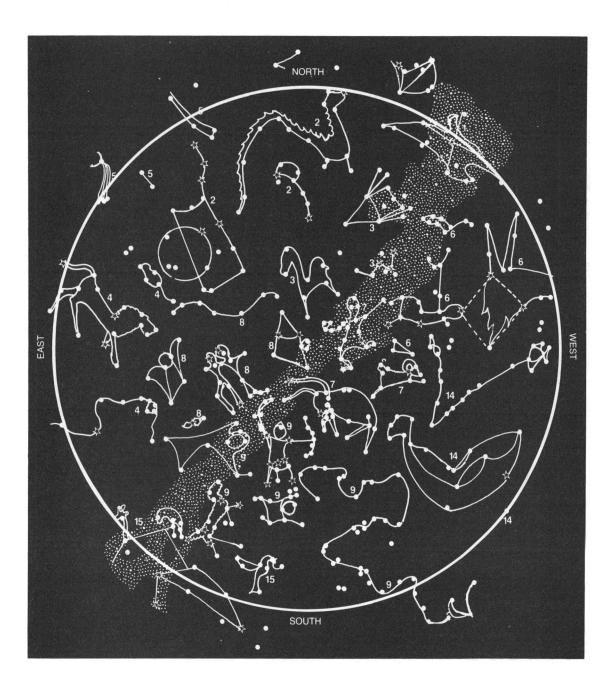

February 1: 7-9 p.m.

To adjust for differing date or hour, see instructions on page 118.

WHOLE SKY CHART 3

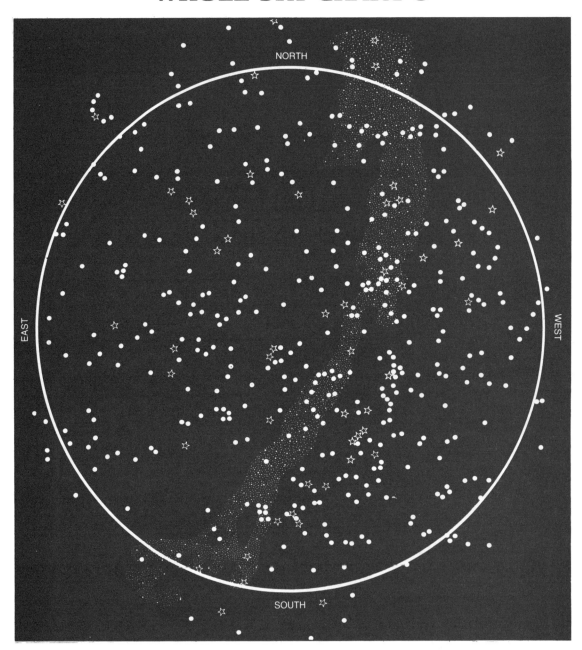

NORTH

EAST

WEST

SOUTH

☆ Stars of first- or
  second-magnitudes (or brighter)

● All stars of lesser magnitude

Numbers in chart at right refer
to Constellation Charts 1-17.

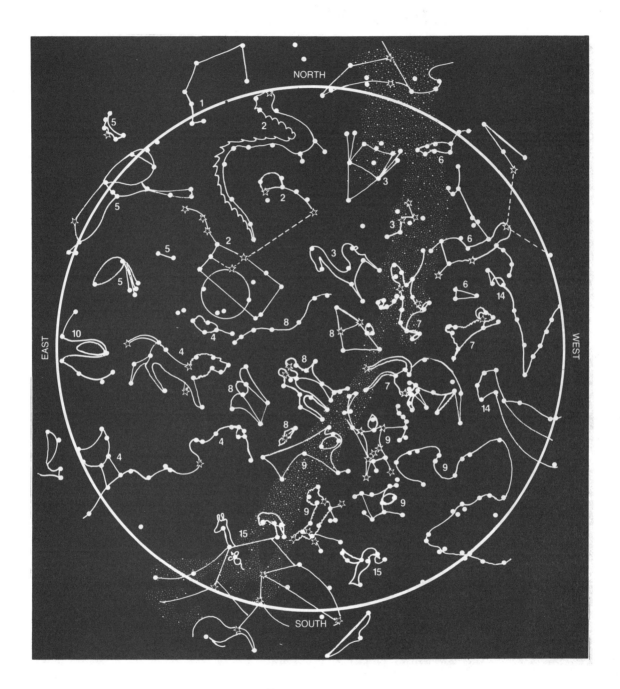

March 1: 7-9 p.m.

To adjust for differing date or hour, see instructions on page 118.

WHOLE SKY CHART 4

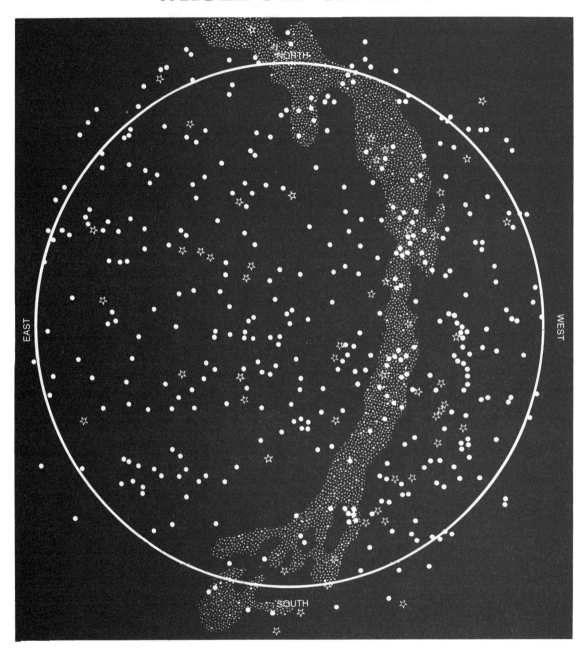

☆ Stars of first- or
   second-magnitudes (or brighter)

● All stars of lesser magnitude

Numbers in chart at right refer
to Constellation Charts 1-17.

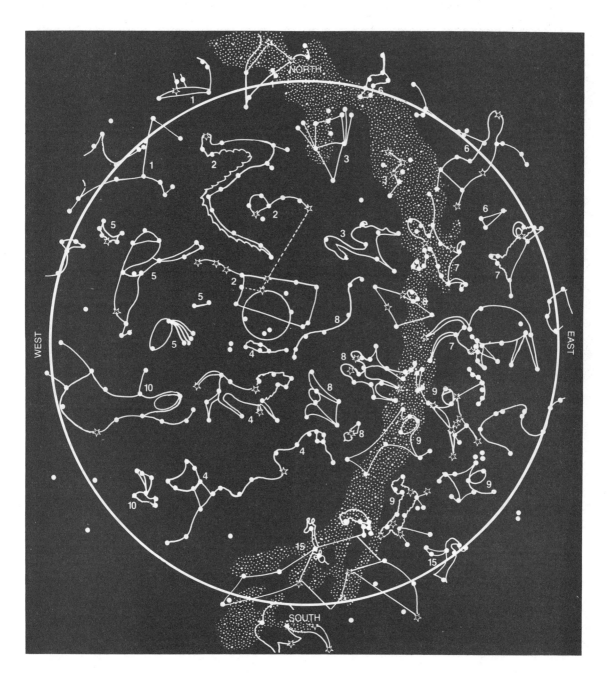

April 1: 7-9 p.m.

To adjust for differing date or hour, see instructions on page 118.

WHOLE SKY CHART 5

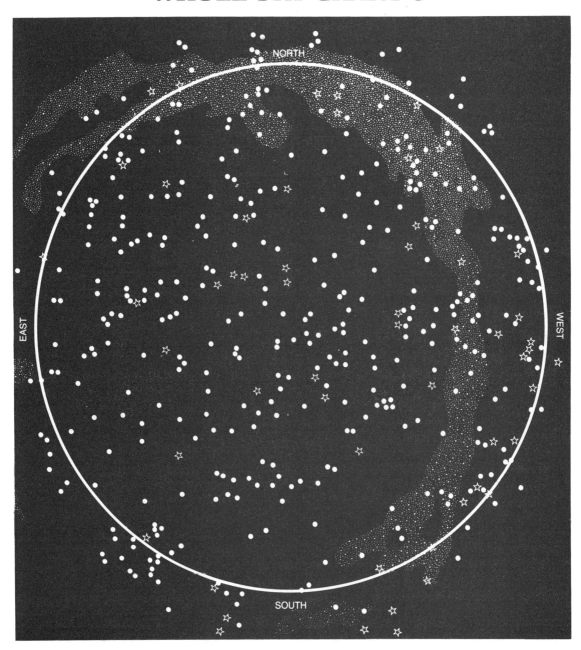

☆ Stars of first- or
   second-magnitudes (or brighter)
● All stars of lesser magnitude

Numbers in chart at right refer
to Constellation Charts 1-17.

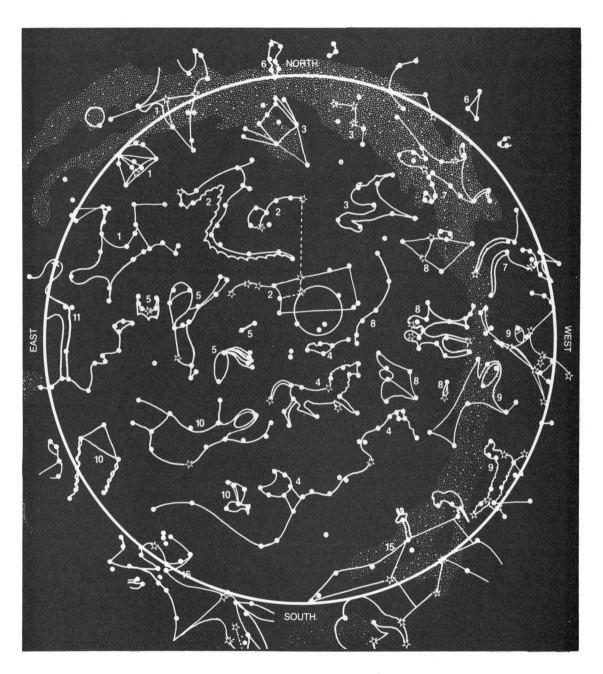

May 1: 7-9 p.m.

To adjust for differing date or hour, see instructions on page 118.

WHOLE SKY CHART 6

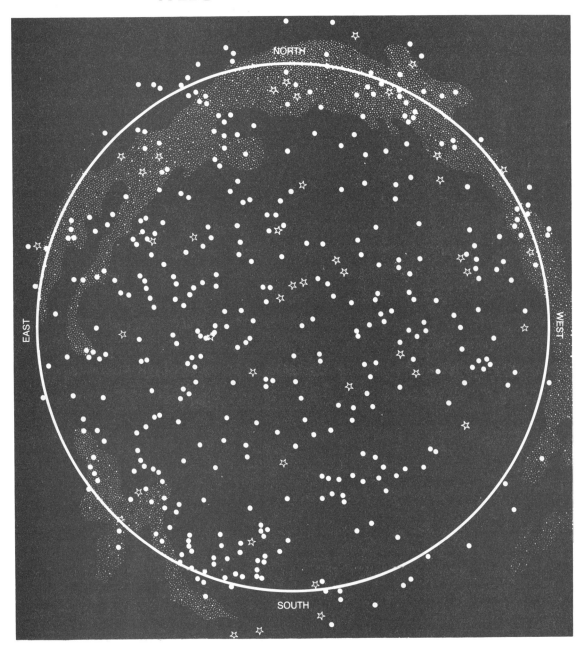

☆ Stars of first- or
  second-magnitudes (or brighter)

● All stars of lesser magnitude

Numbers in chart at right refer
to Constellation Charts 1-17.

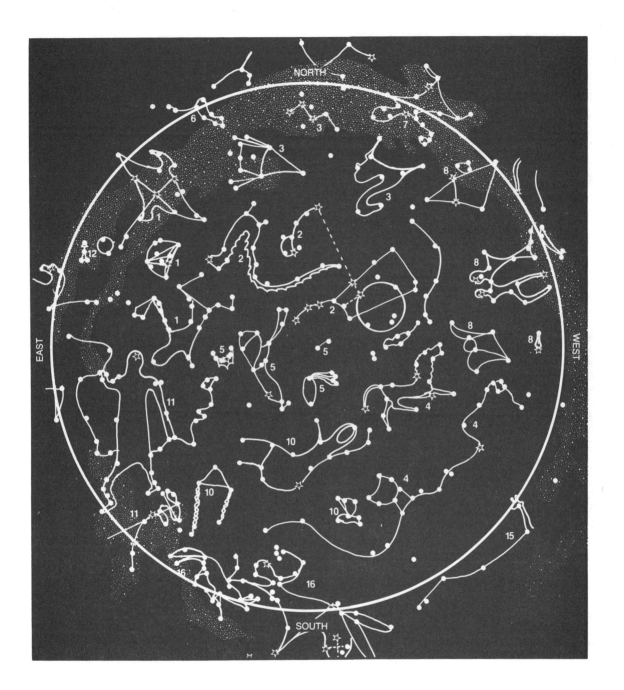

June 1: 7-9 p.m.

To adjust for differing date or hour, see instructions on page 118.

WHOLE SKY CHART 7

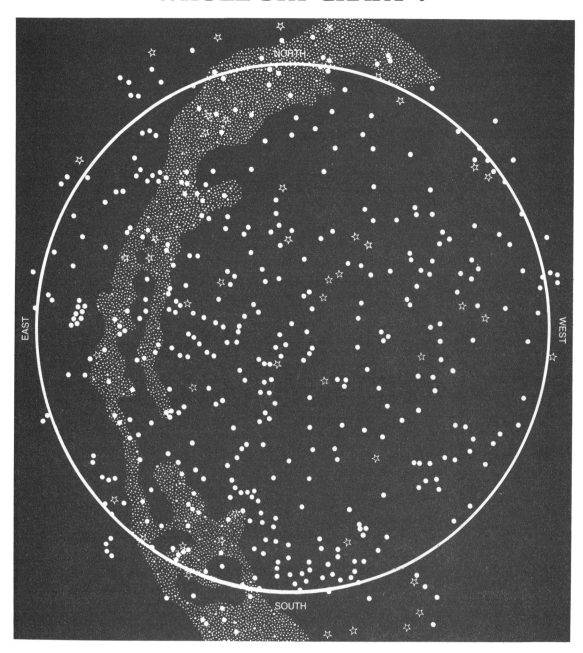

☆ Stars of first- or
   second-magnitudes (or brighter)
● All stars of lesser magnitude

Numbers in chart at right refer
to Constellation Charts 1-17.

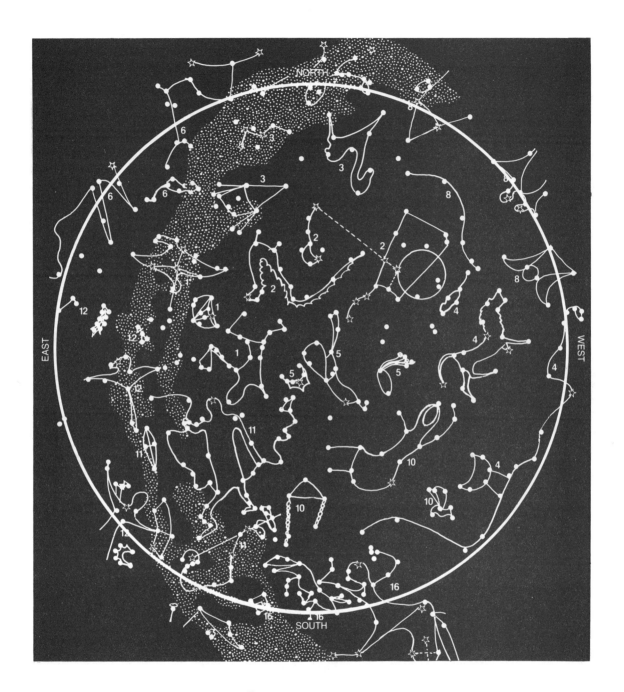

July 1: 7-9 p.m.

To adjust for differing date or hour, see instructions on page 118.

WHOLE SKY CHART 8

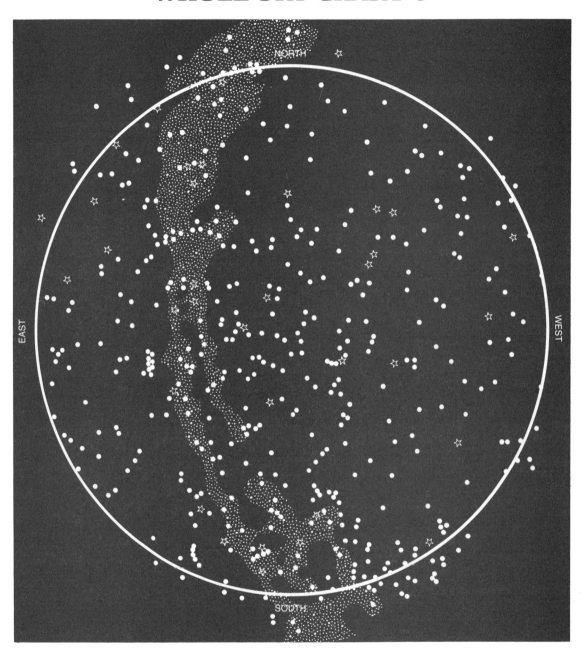

NORTH

EAST

WEST

SOUTH

☆ Stars of first- or
   second-magnitudes (or brighter)

● All stars of lesser magnitude

Numbers in chart at right refer
to Constellation Charts 1-17.

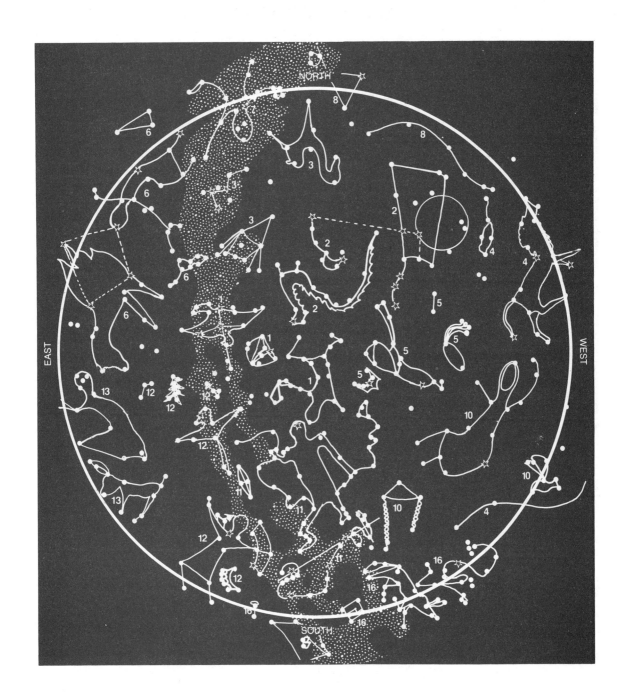

August 1: 7-9 p.m.

To adjust for differing date or hour, see instructions on page 118.

WHOLE SKY CHART 9

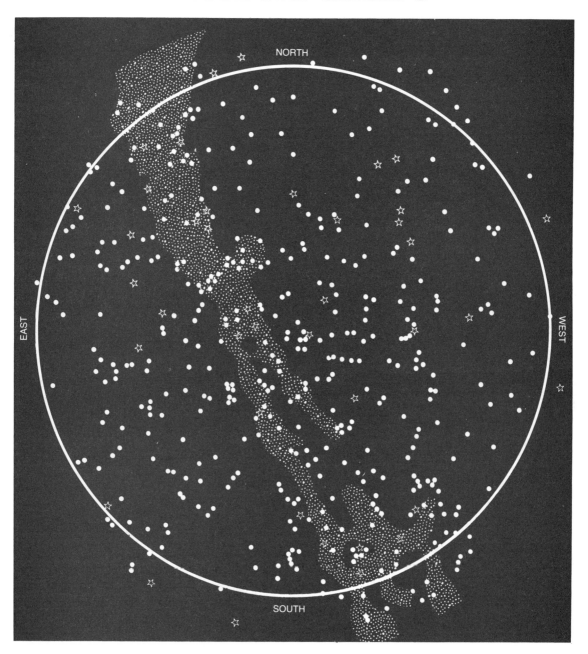

NORTH

EAST

WEST

SOUTH

☆ Stars of first- or
 second-magnitudes (or brighter)

● All stars of lesser magnitude

Numbers in chart at right refer
to Constellation Charts 1-17.

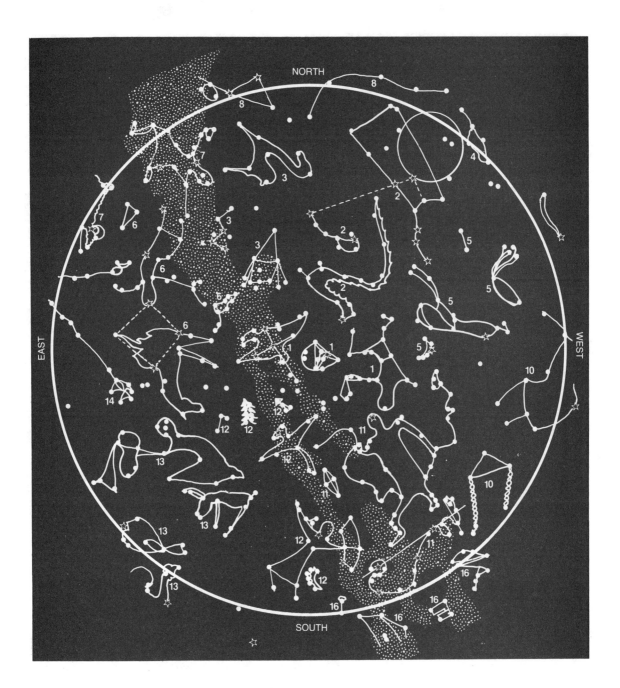

September 1: 7-9 p.m.

To adjust for differing date or hour, see instructions on page 118.

137

WHOLE SKY CHART 10

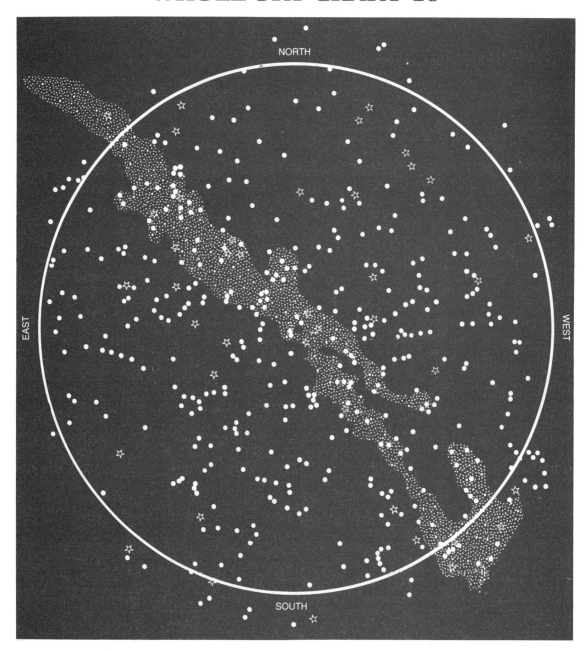

NORTH

EAST

WEST

SOUTH

☆ Stars of first- or
second-magnitudes (or brighter)

● All stars of lesser magnitude

Numbers in chart at right refer
to Constellation Charts 1-17.

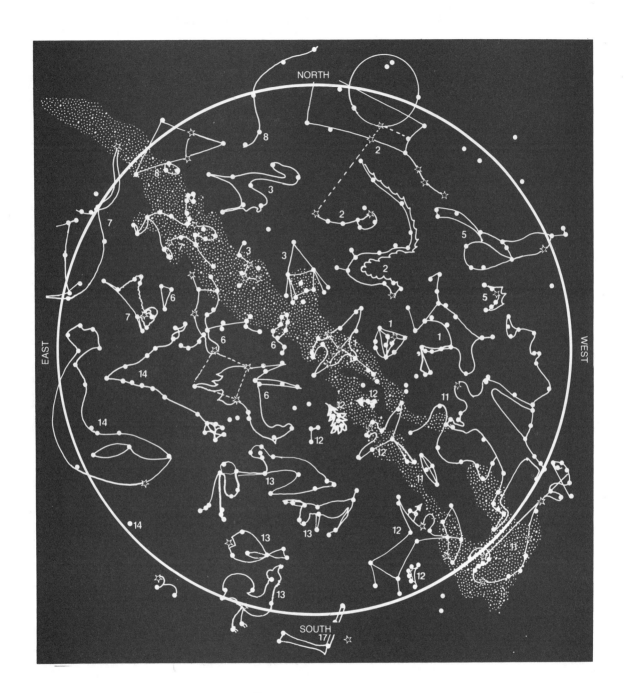

October 1: 7-9 p.m.

To adjust for differing date or hour, see instructions on page 118.

WHOLE SKY CHART 11

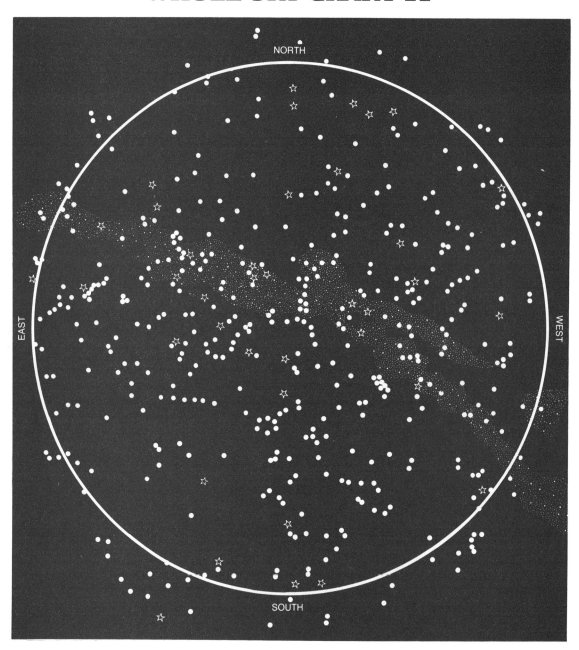

☆ Stars of first- or
 second-magnitudes (or brighter)

● All stars of lesser magnitude

Numbers in chart at right refer
to Constellation Charts 1-17.

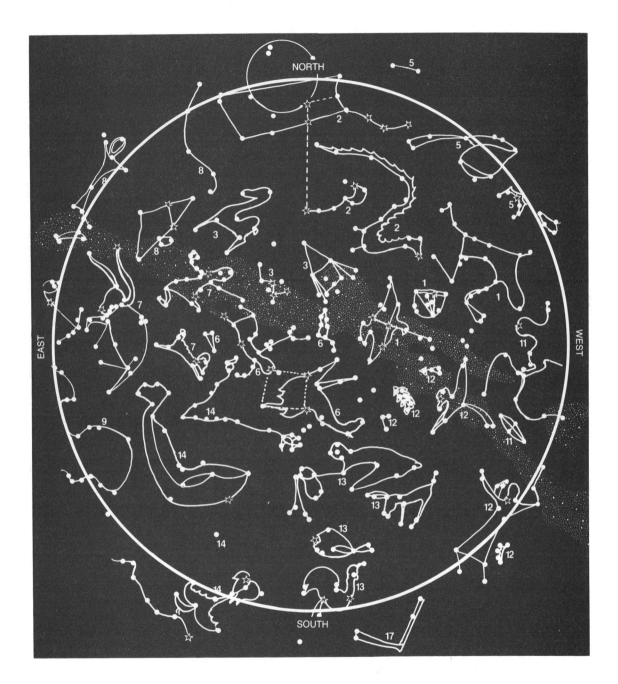

November 1: 7-9 p.m.

To adjust for differing date or hour, see instructions on page 118.

WHOLE SKY CHART 12

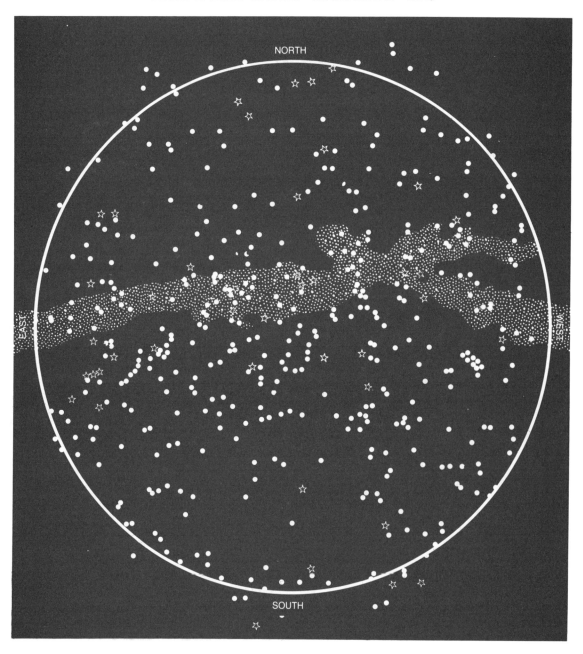

☆ Stars of first- or
   second-magnitudes (or brighter)

● All stars of lesser magnitude

Numbers in chart at right refer
to Constellation Charts 1-17.

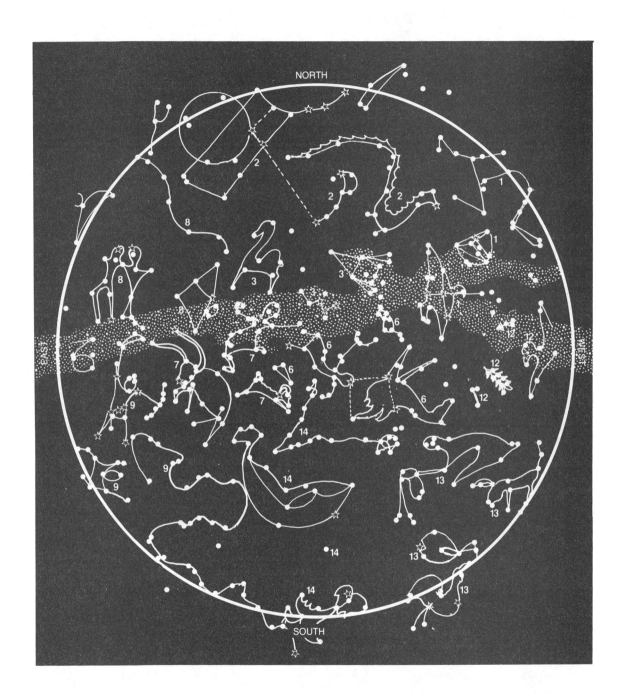

December 1: 7-9 p.m.

To adjust for differing date or hour, see instructions on page 118.

143

IV

WHERE DO WE GO FROM HERE?

The Greatest Lesson of All

We've come to the end of a journey—through the skies, through history, and through the Bible. It may be a long time before you know your way around all these constellations easily, but you now have a useful map to guide you.

You have seen that the patterns of the stars can be viewed in many ways. Some constellations have had more names from around the world than we can remember, each one different and interesting. They remind us that the human imagination is a rich gift from God. To use it for his glory, we need to keep it stretched—and the night sky is a good place for exercise.

If you're interested in learning more about the stars, you'll be happy to know that there's much more information available in other books. Some of these are listed in the back of this volume. We've had no room here to talk much about the moon, our solar system, or our galaxy as a whole. We never even mentioned black holes, quasars, or other mysteries of the universe. But if you make good use of your local library, you can keep learning about the heavens.

Today our most powerful telescopes can see more than five *billion* light-years into space. Out there are hundreds of millions of galaxies, each containing billions of suns. Between these galaxies are millions of light-years of empty blackness.

If that is a frightening thought, we need only remember the One who made it all. Our little globe may be spinning in a corner of the galaxy that seems lost in the vastness of so much matter and space. But because of Jesus, we can be sure that God loved us enough to join us on this planet for a season.

At the end of this journey through the stars, we've come to see in a new way that the heavens declare the glory of God, and the love of God as well. That's the greatest lesson we could have learned. Even on the darkest of nights, the testimony of the stars can comfort us. For every last one of those brilliant lights, the Bible tells us, God has counted and named. And every last light-year of space, with all that is in it, he holds with care in the palm of his hand.

V
APPENDICES

THE TWENTY-ONE BRIGHTEST STARS IN THE SKY

These are given in order of brightness. The lower the magnitude, the brighter the star. Also given here are color and the constellation where the star can be found.

Sirius in the Lamb of God; mag. -1.42; blue
Canopus in Noah's Ark; mag. -9.72; yellow-white
Alpha Centauri in Paul's Vision; mag. -0.27; yellow-orange
Arcturus in Joshua; mag.-0.06; orange
Vega in David's Lyre; mag. 0.03; blue-white
Capella in Sarah's Tent; mag. 0.09; yellow
Rigel in Goliath; mag. 0.15; blue-white
Procyon in the Flaming Sword; mag. 035; yellow-white
Achernar in the Jordan River; mag. 0.49; blue
Beta Centauri in Paul's Vision; mag. 061; blue
Betelgeuse in Goliath; mag. 0.69; red
Altair in the Eagle; mag. 074; yellow-white
Aldebaran in Gideon's Bull; mag. 0.86; orange
Acrux (Alpha Crucis) in Paul's Vision; mag. 0.87; blue
Antares in the Bronze Serpent; mag. 0.89; red
Spica in Mary's Song; mag. 0.96; blue
Pollux in Adam and Eve; mag. 1.13; yellow
Fomalhaut in the Fish with the Coin; mag. 1.16; blue-white
Deneb in the Cross; mag. 1.25; white
Becrux (Beta Crucis) in Paul's Vision; mag. 1.28; blue
Regulus in Daniel's Lions; mag. 1.35; blue-white

ALPHABETIC LIST OF THE OFFICIAL CONSTELLATION NAMES

Andromeda, the Woman in Chains (Peter in Prison)

Antlia, the Pump (not used)

Apus, the Bird of Paradise (the Locust in the Plagues of Egypt)

Aquarius, the Water Carrier (Jesus the Servant)

Aquila, the Eagle (the Eagle)

Ara, the Altar (Solomon's Temple)

Aries, the Ram (Abraham's Ram)

Auriga, the Charioteer (Sarah's Tent)

Bootes, the Herdsman (Joshua)

Caelum, the Chisel (not used)

Camelopardalis, the Giraffe (Rebekah's Camel)

Cancer, the Crab (the Angel)

Canes Venatici, the Hunting Dogs (Nimrod's Dogs)

Canis Major, the Big Dog (the Lamb of God)

Canis Minor, the Little Dog (the Flaming Sword)

Capricornus, the Sea Goat (Balaam's Donkey)

Carina, the Ship's Keel (part of Noah's Ark)

Cassiopeia, the Queen (the Stormy Sea)

Centaurus, the Centaur (Paul's Vision)

Cepheus, the King (the Tabernacle)

Cetus, the Sea Monster (Jonah's Great Fish)

Chamaeleon, the Chameleon (the Frog in the Plagues of Egypt)

Circinus, the Compass (the Hammer in Joseph's Tools)

Columba, the Dove (the Dove in Noah's Ark)

Coma Berenices, Berenice's Hair (Samson's Hair)

Corona Australis, the Southern Crown (Stephen's Crown)

Corona Borealis, the Northern Crown (Esther's Crown)

Corvus, the Crow (Elijah's Raven)

Crater, the Cup (the Communion Cup)

Crux, the [Southern] Cross (the donkey's face in Paul's Vision)

Cygnus, the Swan (the Cross with the dove of the Holy Spirit)

Delphinus, the Dolphin (the Palm Branch)

Dorado, the Dolphin (the Lamp)

Draco, the Dragon (the Dragon)

Equuleus, the Colt (the Palm Sunday colt beside the Palm Branch)

Eridanus, the River Eridanus (the Jordan River)

Gemini, the Twins (Adam and Eve)

Grus, the Crane (Peter's Rooster)

Hercules, the Strongman (King of Kings)

Horologium, the Clock (not used)

Hydra, the Water Serpent (the Snake)

Hydrus, The Male Water Serpent (the Empty Tomb)

Indus, the Indian (Elisha's Ax)

Lacerta, the Lizard (the Lizard in Peter in Prison)

Leo, the Lion (the larger Lion in Daniel's Lions)

Leo Minor, the Little Lion (the smaller Lion in Daniel's Lions)

Lepus, the Hare (the Shield Bearer alongside Goliath)

Libras, the Scales (Belshazzar's Scales)

Lupus, the Wolf (Benjamin's Wolf)

Lynx, the Lynx (Lydia's River)

Lyra, the Lyre (David's Lyre)

Mensa, the Table Mountain (not used)

Microscopium, the Microscope (not used)

Monoceros, the Unicorn (Ruth)

Musca, the Fly (the Fly in the Plagues of Egypt)

Norma [et Regula], the Square [and Level] (the Square and Level in Joseph's Tools)

Octas, the Octant (the Saw in Joseph's Tools)

Ophiuchus, the Serpent Holder (Paul and the Viper)

Orion, the Hunter (Goliath)

Pavo, the Peacock (the Coat of Many Colors)

Pegasus, the Winged Horse (the Fiery Horse)

Perseus, the Hero (David)

Phoenix, the Phoenix (the Phoenix)

Pictor, the Easel (the Plane in Joseph's Tools)

Pisces, the Fish (the Multiplied Fishes)

Piscis Austrinus, the Southern Fish (the Fish with the Coin)

Puppis, the Ship's Stern (part of Noah's Ark)

Pyxis, the Ship's Compass (part of Noah's Ark)

Reticulum, the Net (the Disciples' Net)

Sagitta, the Arrow (Jonathan's Arrow)

Sagittarius, the Archer (Esau)

Scorpius, the Scorpion (the Bronze Serpent)

Sculptor, the Sculptor (the worm in Jonah's Great Fish)

Scutum, the Shield (the Shield of Faith)

Serpens Caput, the Serpent's Head (the viper's head in Paul and the Viper)

Serpens Cauda, the Serpent's Tail (the viper's tail in Paul and the Viper)

Sextans, the Sextant (not used)

Taurus, the Bull (Gideon's Bull)

Telescopium, the Telescope (the Nail in Joseph's Tools)

Triangulum, the Triangle (the Holy Trinity)

Triangulum Australe, the Southern Triangle (the Tower of Babel)

Tucana, the Toucan (the Anchor of Hope)

Ursa Major, the Great Bear (Pharaoh's Chariot)

Ursa Minor, the Little Bear (the Living Water)

Vela, the Ship's Sail (part of Noah's Ark)

Virgo, the Virgin (Mary's Song)

Volans, the Flying Fish (Deborah's Palm)

Vulpecula, the Little Fox (the Fox's Hole)

THE TWELVE CONSTELLATIONS OF THE ZODIAC

These are the twelve constellations through which the sun, moon, and planets travel in their path across the sky through the year. Starting with Abraham's Ram and moving east:

Abraham's Ram (official name, Aries)

Gideon's Bull (Taurus)

Adam and Eve (Gemini)

The Angel (Cancer)

Daniel's Lions (Leo)

Mary's Song (Virgo)

Belshazzar's Scales (Libra)

The Bronze Serpent (Scorpius)

Esau (Sagittarius)

Balaam's Donkey (Capricornus)

John the Baptist (Aquarius)

The Multiplied Fishes (Pisces)

ALPHABETIC LIST OF THE BIBLICAL CONSTELLATION NAMES

The numbers in bold give the constellation chart where the group is featured; the other numbers are the pages where the constellation is described or mentioned.

Abraham's Ram (*Aries*) **7;** 68, 69
Adam and Eve (*Gemini*) **8;** 71, 73
The Anchor of Hope (*Tucana*) **17;** 111
The Angel (*Cancer*) **8;** 71, 73

Balaam's Donkey (*Capricornus*) **13;** 93, 95
Belshazzar's Scales (*Libra*) **10;** 81, 82
Benjamin's Wolf (*Lupus*) **16;** 107
The Bronze Serpent (*Scorpius*) **11;** 85, 86

The Coat of Many Colors (*Pavo*) **17;** 109
The Communion Cup (*Crater*) **4;** 57
The Cross [and the dove of the Holy Spirit] (*Cygnus*) **1;** 41, 43

Daniel's Lions (*Leo, Leo Minor*) **4;** 53, 57
David (*Perseus*) **7;** 67, 69
David's Lyre (*Lyra*) **1;** 41, 43
Deborah's Palm (*Volans*) **15;** 102
The Disciples' Net (*Reticulum*) **15;** 103
The Dragon (*Draco*) **2;** 45, 48, 52

The Eagle (*Aquila*) **12;** 87, 91
Elijah's Raven (*Corvus*) **10;** 82
Elisha's Ax (*Indus*) **17;** 111
The Empty Tomb (*Hydrus*) **17;** 111
Esau (*Sagittarius*) **12;** 89, 91
Esther's Crown (*Corona Borealis*) **15;** 59, 61

The Fiery Horse (*Pegasus*) **6;** 64, 65
The Fish with the Coin (*Piscis Austrinus*) **13;** 94, 95
The Flaming Sword (*Canis Minor*) **8;** 71, 73
The Fox's Hole (*Vulpecula*) **12;** 90, 91

Gideon's Bull (*Taurus*) **7;** 67, 69
Goliath [with his Shield-Bearer] (*Orion, Lepus*) **9;** 37, 75, 76, 79

The Holy Trinity (*Triangulum*) **6;** 65

Jesus the Servant (*Aquarius*) **13;** 93, 95
Jonah's Great Fish [with the worm] (*Cetus, Sculptor*) **14;** 97, 99
Jonathan's Arrow (*Sagitta*) **12;** 89, 91
The Jordan River (*Eridanus*) **9;** 78, 79

Joseph's Tools [Compass, Square and Level, Saw, Plane, Nail] (*Circinus, Norma [et Regula], Octans, Pictor, Telescopium*) **15, 16;** 102, 103, 105
Joshua (*Bootes*) **5;** 59, 61

King of Kings (*Hercules*) **1;** 42, 43, 45

The Lamb of God (*Canis Major*) **9;** 76, 79
The Lamp (*Dorado*) **15;** 103
The Living Water (*Ursa Minor*) **2;** 45, 48, 52
Lydia's River (*Lynx*) **8;** 73

Mary's Song (*Virgo*) **10;** 81, 82
The Multiplied Fishes (*Pisces*) **14;** 97, 99

Nimrod's Dogs (*Canes Venatici*) **5;** 59, 61
Noah's Ark [with the Dove] (*Carina, Columba, Puppis, Pyxis, Vela*) **15;** 101

The Palm Branch [with the Colt] (*Delphinus, Equuleus*) **12;** 90, 91
Paul and the Viper (*Ophiucus, Serpens Caput, Serpens Cauda*) **11;** 83, 86
Paul's Vision (*Centaurus, Crux*) **16;** 105
Peter in Prison [with the lizard] (*Andromeda, Lacerta*) **6;** 63, 65
Peter's Rooster (*Grus*) **13;** 95
Pharaoh's Chariot (*Ursa Major*) **2;** 46, 47, 48, 52
The Phoenix (*Phoenix*) **14;** 99
The Plagues of Egypt [Locust, Frog, Fly] (*Apus, Chamaeleon, Musca*) **16;** 106

Rebekah's Camel (*Camelopardalis*) **3;** 51, 52
Ruth (*Monoceros*) **9;** 78, 79

Samson's Hair (*Coma Berenices*) **5;** 60, 61
Sarah's Tent (*Auriga*) **8;** 72, 73
The Shield of Faith (*Scutum*) **11;** 86
The Snake (*Hydra*) **4;** 57
Solomon's Temple (*Ara*) **16;** 108
Stephen's Crown (*Corona Australis*) **12;** 91
The Stormy Sea (*Cassiopeia*) **3;** 49, 52

The Tabernacle (*Cepheus*) **3;** 51, 52
The Tower of Babel (*Triangulum Australe*) **16;** 105

BIBLE VERSES THAT MENTION THE STARS

Genesis 1:16; 15:5; 22:17; 26:4; 37:9

Exodus 32:13

Numbers 24:17

Deuteronomy 1:10; 4:19; 10:22; 17:3; 28:62

Judges 5:20

II Kings 17:16; 21:3, 5; 23:4, 5

I Chronicles 27:23

II Chronicles 33:3-5

Nehemiah 4:21; 9:6, 23

Job 3:9; 9:7-9; 22:12; 25:5; 38:7, 31, 32

Psalms 8:3; 19:1; 33:6; 136:9; 147:4; 148:3

Ecclesiastes 12:2

Song of Solomon 6:10

Isaiah 13:10; 14:12, 13; 34:4; 40:26; 45:12; 47:13

Jeremiah 8:2; 19:13; 31:35; 33:22

Ezekiel 32:7

Daniel 8:10; 12:3

Joel 2:10; 3:15

Amos 5:8, 26

Obadiah 4

Nahum 3:16

Zephaniah 1:5

Matthew 2:2-10; 24:29

Mark 13:25

Luke 21:25, 26

Acts 7:42, 43; 27:20

I Corinthians 15:40, 41

Philippians 2:15

Hebrews 11:12

II Peter 1:19

Jude 13

Revelation 1:16, 20; 2:1, 28; 3:1; 6:13; 8:10-12; 9:1; 12:1, 4; 22:16

FOR FURTHER READING

A number of excellent books on astronomy are available if you want to learn more. Here are a few, including some that were most important in research for this book.

Allen, Richard Hinckly, *Star Names: Their Lore and Meaning*. New York: Dover, 1963.

Branley, Franklyn Mansfield. *A Book of Stars for You*. New York: Thomas Y. Crowell, 1965.

—*The Sky Is Full of Stars*. New York: Thomas Y. Crowell, 1981.

Chartrand, Mark R. *Skyguide: A Field Guide for Amateur Astronomers*. New York: Golden Press, 1982.

Dreyer, J. L. E. *A History of Astronomy*. New York: Dover, 1953.

Gallant, Roy A. *The Constellations: How They Came to Be*. New York: Four Winds Press, 1979.

—*The Planets: Exploring the Solar System*. New York: Four Winds Press, 1982.

Herbst, Judith. *Sky Above and Worlds Beyond*. New York: Atheneum, 1983.

Rey, H. A. *Find the Constellations*. Boston: Houghton Mifflin, 1976.

—*The Stars: A New Way to See Them*. Boston: Houghton Mifflin, 1976.

Weiss, Malcolm E. *Sky Watchers of Ages Past*. Boston: Houghton Mifflin, 1982.

GLOSSARY

ASTROLOGER, someone who practices the false science of astrology.

ASTROLOGY, a false science claiming to foretell the future, and determine the characteristics of individuals, by studying the supposed influence of heavenly bodies on human affairs. Astrology is condemned in the Bible as an abomination to God.

ASTRONOMY, the science of the stars, planets, and all other heavenly bodies, dealing with their composition, motion, relative position, and size.

ASTRONOMER, an expert in astronomy.

BINARY STAR, two stars revolving around each other, relatively close together. DOUBLE STAR.

CIRCUMPOLAR CONSTELLATIONS, the six constellations that are arranged closest around the Polestar, and are always above the horizon in middle and northern latitudes: Pharaoh's Chariot, The Stormy Sea, the Living Water, the Tabernacle, the Dragon, and Rebekah's Camel.

COAL SACKS, dark spots in the Milky Way caused by clouds of cosmic dust which hide the stars, also called a *dark nebula*. See also NEBULA.

CONSTELLATION, a grouping of stars that makes up some pattern which can be recognized. There are 88 "official" constellations which have been recognized by international agreement. (See Appendix Two.)

ECLIPTIC, the path among the stars which the sun appears to take over the course of a year; it runs through the middle of the zodiac. See also ZODIAC.

GALAXY, a vast system of stars, typically containing between a million and a trillion stars, plus other material such as dust and gas. Our own galaxy, the Milky Way, has about a hundred billion stars. See also MILKY WAY.

GIANT STAR, a star between 10 and 100 times the diameter of the sun. See also SUPERGIANT STAR.

KEYSTONE, the four stars which form a keystone shape in the body of the King of Kings; useful in finding this constellation.

LIGHT-YEAR, unit of measurement for distances in space, equal to about 6 trillion miles. The distance light travels in a year through a vacuum—that is, without any matter in the way to slow it down.

LUMINOSITY, total amount of energy released from a star per unit of time; the power output of a star.

MAGELLANIC CLOUDS, two galaxies which move around the Milky Way as satellites. They appear near the sky's south pole, close to the Lamp and the Empty Tomb constellations.

MAGNITUDE, brightness of a star as it appears in our sky; the lower the magnitude, the brighter the star.

MILKY WAY, faint band of starlight seen stretching across the sky on a clear, moonless night. Made up of the combined light of millions of stars too faint to be seen individually with the unaided eye. Milky Way is also the name we give to the galaxy of which our sun is a part (see GALAXY). This galaxy is shaped like a disk; but it appears as a band of light in the sky because we are looking out at it sideways.

NEBULA (plural, NEBULAE), a cloud of gas and dust visible either as a shining region or a dark patch against the background of stars.

POLESTAR, a second-magnitude star near the north pole of the sky, useful for finding directions and locating other stars. It remains almost always exactly north in the sky. POLARIS; NORTH STAR.

SUPERGIANT STAR, a star which is more than 100 times the diameter of the sun. See also GIANT STAR.

SUPERNOVA (plural, SUPERNOVAE), a star which flares up rapidly into extreme brightness, and then fades away. Supernovae appear to be stars which explode and blow themselves apart.

VARIABLE STAR, a star whose brightness varies. Reasons for the change also vary. Some are binary stars which grow dim when the dimmer of the two stars eclipses the brighter one. Others vary in brightness because of some process going on inside the star itself.

ZODIAC, a belt across the sky formed by twelve constellations. These are the background area through which the sun, moon, and planets appear to move throughout the year. For a list, see Appendix Five.

INDEX

For a list of the official constellation names and their biblical equivalents, see pages 152-153. For a list of biblical constellation names, and the charts and pages where they appear, see page 154.